Susanna Wesley

Susanna Wesley

by

Sandy Dengler

MOODY PRESS

CHICAGO

Library of Congress Cataloging in Publication Data

Dengler, Sandy.
  Susanna Wesley.

  Summary: Follows the life of the Englishwoman whose intellectual curiosity led her to study theology, who married a minister who hoped to bring revival to the Anglican Church, and who lived to embrace the Methodism founded by her son John Wesley.
  1. Wesley, Susanna Annesley, 1670-1742—Juvenile literature. 2. Methodists—England—Biography—Juvenile literature. 3. Anglicans—England—Biography—Juvenile literature. 4. Wesley, John, 1703-1791—Family—Juvenile literature. 5. Wesley, Charles, 1707-1788—Family—Juvenile literature. [1. Wesley, Susanna Annesley, 1670-1742. 2. Methodists] I. Title.
BX8495.W55D46 1987   287'.092'4 [B] [92]   87-5666
ISBN 0-8024-8414-X

10

Contents

1

Pretty Sukey

When bitter gusts out of the north hammer London, the tightest window cannot keep the penetrating cold at bay. Most of the year, thick and murky overcasts seal out the sun and seal in the acrid smoke of a hundred thousand chimneys. Silent, clammy fog can, for days on end, hide the front door from the cobbled street hard before it. Then suddenly, when you least expect it, the sun slips out to burn the chill away.

If you pass the Bear Garden during an entertainment, when dogs are baiting bears and bulls, you can watch dust and the steamy breath of all those screaming people rise above the round arena in the smoky torchlight. Then it's over. The bulls and the bears and some of the dogs are dead; and the hot, sweaty patrons, laughing and shouting and drinking, come pouring out into the cold, rain-slick streets.

Weather happens inside, too. The vast, echoing sanctuary of St. Giles chills the marrow of your bones any day of the year. The walk-in hearth in Spital Fields manse, so richly warm, welcomes you with a crackling wood fire, or possibly the soft and gentle glow of burning peat. Hot and cold, sun and wind, fire and rain, and you never quite know which will come down upon you next.

Today was sun. It filtered through the tree leaves to weave dancing lace in the grass. It made more vivid the crisp green of the sweetbriers along the back fence and made still softer the quiet pink of their fragrant flowers. It sang for the joy of another English summer.

Out back in the courtyard, the upstairs maid had hung out the rug from the master bedroom. With loud and mighty *whops* she rhythmically slapped it with the broom. A little cloud of dust lifted away from each swat. The houseman was finally replacing those three broken sticks in the arching rose arbor. The two tame cats had cornered something small and squeaky in the pile of kindling outside the kitchen door. The chore girl turned her back on the cat-rodent brouhaha to polish the big brass dinner bell hanging by the back stoop. And over all poured that delicious yellow sunlight.

"Sukey, for pity sake! Throw that musty old book aside and come out in the sun. The weather's much too fine to hide from!"

Susanna didn't throw it aside; she laid it down carefully. She leaned out her upstairs casement window. There stood Elizabeth in the busy courtyard below, her lovely face tipped up into the brightness, arms akimbo. Should Susanna be properly deferential toward her older sister, or should Susanna be as usual? As usual, of course.

She had to pause and think a moment. *"Deus deorum Dominus locutus est: et vocavit terram, a solis ortu usque ad occasum."*

"Whaaat?"

"Psalm fifty, verse one. You see? You can study and improve your mind, or you can bask in the sun like a lizard. I choose study. Bask as you wish."

"You're much too saucy for your own good, little snippet. You think you know it all, but you're only thirteen, remember."

"Better thirteen than on the brink of marriage. Enjoy your sunshine, Elizabeth. Too soon you'll be confined to the house scrubbing floors and birthing babies." Susanna pulled her head back inside and let the not-so-polite language from below drift by unheeded. And Elizabeth the daughter of a rector, too! Smugly she settled back onto her bolster beside the window. She picked up the musty old book again.

Musty? Old? Good! Both words bespoke venerability, the wisdom of age. Susanna yearned for the wisdom of age. Blessed she was indeed to have a brilliant father with a huge library and smart sisters willing to help her learn.

Oh, true, the rest of London called the Annesley sisters pretty, as if pretty were the best thing a girl could be. They called Susanna, the youngest, the prettiest of all and constantly complimented

9

her silky dark hair, her deep blue eyes. Why didn't the people who visited the manse here ever notice that Susanna like her sisters could read Hebrew, Greek, and Latin, could cipher as well as any man, could discuss theology with any seminarian? Those were accomplishments worthy of pride, not an accident of birth, such as physical beauty.

Like a siren's soft fluting, warm summer air pushed aside the musty aroma of books to beckon and tease. The book melted into her lap. Perhaps Elizabeth had a point. Why waste all this fine weather? Susanna laid her study gently aside and walked downstairs. The long hallway ticked quietly in rhythm with her heels.

"Sukey? Have you a minute?"

"For you, Papa, many minutes," Susanna paused in the doorway of her father's study. She knew what the topic was going to be, and she wished it weren't. She crossed the cozy room and settled at her father's feet. His knees and his huge padded armchair like a throne towered above her.

He sat back and laced his thick fingers together in that way of his. "I was over in the City yesterday. St. Paul's is coming, but quite slowly. Some say it'll be many years more a-building, and I believe them."

"I wish I could have seen it before the fire. They say you could spy its steeple from fifty miles away, if the land lay right." Susanna squirmed. St. Paul's Cathedral wasn't the subject of this chat. "And the fire must have been interesting. Sammy and Benny tell me stories about it, but I never know quite when to believe them, they tease so much. I was born three years too late."

"Ah. Now my littlest daughter is questioning God's sovereign timing."

"Very well then, Papa. Not questioning it. Regretting it."

"And what else do you regret about God's sovereignty?"

"That's not fair, Papa. I don't argue against His sovereignty, but I do have wishes. I wish girls could attend academies and seminaries as boys do. I wish people took me more seriously. I wish— I wish Elizabeth weren't marrying John Dunton. I see him as boastful and full of self; not altogether a man to God's liking."

Her father studied her from his throne. "This from a slip of a girl who's not yet seen fourteen winters? You know what God likes and doesn't like?"

"His Word is clear."

"And you think He likes the Church of England."

She'd been right. Here was the topic she dreaded. How should she phrase her arguments this time? She drew her knees up tight against her chest and folded her arms across them, a chin-rest.

"Papa—" She refolded her arms. They felt no more comfortable than before. "Papa—" she sighed "—I don't blame God that I can't attend Oxford or some such college; I blame men. They set those rules. And I don't blame God for the injuries you suffered at the hands of church officials.

11

That also is the work of men. Petty men, preying upon a great one."

"I've warned you against flattery, Sukey."

"Not flattery, Papa. Your life speaks for itself. The people you serve in your congregation, the way students and young men revere you. You are great among the unconformists, and I respect you for that. And for lots of other reasons. But I don't blame the Church of England, either, when some of its men are petty."

"They form the church. They are the church."

"In a way. But in another way the church is a thing herself. It's the thing herself I've pledged allegiance to." Susanna was warming to her topic now; words came easier. "Papa, religion like anything else must have a strong framework of law and order. Hard rules following God's precepts. Your unconformists lack that framework, and the church has it. I feel comfortable in it. I feel comfortable with rules and liturgy. With methodical, proper ways to do things."

Papa smiled down from up there. "You know, my friends tell me you're only a child who doesn't yet know her mind; that you'll come back into worship as we preach it. They think you're frivolous; that you don't understand. Hah! My friends don't know you. They don't take a thirteen-year-old seriously, as you mentioned in your list of wishes, but I do. If that's your choice—to leave my church and go back to the Anglican communion —I'll not condemn you."

"And no more discussion of the topic?"

"Not unless you bring it up."

She curled up against his hard knees, because that was the part of him easiest to reach. "Thank you, Papa. Now what shall we do about Elizabeth?"

Samuel Annesley roared. "That's exactly what Elizabeth says about you! She's always fussing about something you do, as you know. Most lately it's been your involvement with that sect, those Socinians. She's most concerned for your soul, just as you're concerned for her future."

"If the Socinian beliefs are so dangerous, why haven't you preached to me against them?"

"Because you wouldn't listen to me. You follow your own counsel. Always have. I'm trusting the Holy Spirit to bring you around in His good time. He's the teacher. You'll listen to Him eventually, though not to me."

Susanna knew a rebuke when she heard it, however gentle it might be. She dared not answer Papa as she might Elizabeth or brother Benny. So she answered nothing.

"So, Sukey, why aren't you out in this lovely sunshine? No more weighty discussions. Go be a child for a moment."

She sat erect. "I enjoy musty old books and talking religion better than basking. Very well, Papa, here I go. Out to turn brown and shrivel up."

He sat forward on his throne to give her a hug in leaving, and up close here she could see the sadness in his eyes. She hated to hurt this beloved giant so, to turn her back on his church and stray

13

from his beliefs. But she *did* know her own mind, and, certainly more than most her age, she could discern the mind of God. She would walk in the light she saw; after all, that's what her father preached from his pulpit.

She paused in the dining hall a moment to watch the kitchen maid set places for supper. She, being youngest, hardly knew those brothers and sisters who had grown and left the manse. And the brothers and sisters who died in infancy would meet her only in heaven. She measured by eye how long the table would have to be, were all Momma's twenty-five babies alive and still home.

How many babies would Elizabeth bear John Dunton? Susanna shuddered to think. He was so boastful he would probably want to produce babies by the twins and triplets, the better to populate the world with lots of John Duntons. Poor Elizabeth.

On the other hand, the Bible said children were a gift of God and the man who had a quiver full of them was blessed. Hannah, Rachel, Sarah, and a host of other Bible women bitterly bemoaned a lack of children. Her own mother didn't seem to mind giving birth twenty-five times. There might well be something to motherhood that most certainly was not visible from the outside.

Here was Elizabeth at the side gate haggling with the fishmonger. Elizabeth loved to haggle with anyone. Apparently, so did fishmongers. Susanna listened until the exchange started getting shrill and turned her back on the price of salt cod. There had to be more to life than dickering over a few pence for a loaf of barley or a slab of fish.

When she was grown she would never do that. She'd save her arguments for theology in learned circles.

Now there was something she hadn't thought of before. Were all twenty-five of Momma's babies alive and home, what would the food bills be! Talk about haggling over every penny. No, Susanna did not want to be burdened with a large family. Arrows in the quiver might be a blessing to the father of the house but certainly not to the one who did the work. Unless, of course, Susanna married well, as her own mother had.

The two tame cats were stretched out now across the cistern cover, draped in careless attitudes as cats do, as if their bones had melted. Had they caught that mouse? Likely not. The wild cats—the kitties who lived in the stable and tool shed and hid when you came near—they were the mousers.

Susanna stood in the middle of the courtyard and tipped her face up, letting the warmth pour over it. It would definitely have been a mistake to stay inside reading.

Here came Elizabeth with her slab of salt cod, looking quite smug. And there went the fishmonger, looking equally smug as she tucked some coins into the purse at her waist. The cats, so flaccid a moment ago, tensed as they lay there. Their tail tips twitched. With nose and eye and the subtlest turn of the head, they followed the salt cod to the kitchen every step of the way.

Susanna continued her walk. The apple tree would bear well this year. It was dropping tiny

15

green apples all over the path. She wished the manse garden contained a mulberry tree. Why? She didn't know. She simply liked mulberry trees with their rough, broad, no-nonsense leaves and sweet fruit.

She found herself out at the end of the courtyard along the back wall. It was either stop wandering or struggle through sweetbrier to climb a wall with nothing but alley on its other side. She stopped very close to the tangle of sweetbrier. She inhaled deeply and let the warm redolence penetrate her nose and lungs and from there her whole being. Fragrance. Ease and plenty. The good life.

Yes, Susanna Annesley had made up her mind about much more than just a choice of church and a theological doctrine. She also had determined to limit or possibly forgo her childbearing. She might even postpone marriage, maybe forever. Who needed conceited men, anyway? She knew widows and spinsters who did just fine. If she married at all she would marry well, someone highborn yet sensitive, someone with plenty of money. She would certainly never haggle over the price of bread.

Her nose sated with sweet perfume, she took one final deep breath and left the sweetbriers to toast in the sun. She had had sufficient sun and summer for one day. Indeed, she didn't need the sun to feel good. After all, how lucky can a young girl be? At thirteen she already had her theology well established and her life all worked out. Now there was nothing left but to play the orderly scenario to its end.

She clicked down the great hall and up the stairs to her first love, her musty old book.

2

Smart Sam

In theory an unconformist wedding was a simple joining, a mutual exchange of promises before God and man and that was it. But maybe simplicity only works if you're an ordinary person marrying another ordinary person.

Nothing about the Annesley family was ordinary. Papa took under his wing every young dissenting minister in the London area, helping some of them financially and welcoming them all into his home, day or night. He encouraged, exhorted, and edified, then patched up the rifts when his charges got carried away in their many arguments. He preached to hundreds each Sunday and struggled ceaselessly against the established Church of England.

There was nothing ordinary about the Annesley daughters, either. Susanna heard it constantly, sometimes whispered and sometimes openly—how beautiful they were; too clever for their own good;

too indulged in some ways, but their father was after all so indulgent with everyone.

It didn't surprise Susanna, therefore, that Elizabeth's wedding could by no stretch be considered a simple affair. True, there were no robed priests or elaborate rituals. The actual wedding was in fact quite plain. But there were people! Every dissenter in Southwark trooped through the polished halls of the great manse, nibbling from the acre of buffet, laughing, jostling, churning, joking. So many strange faces milled about that Susanna was sure half of the rest of London had come as well.

Elizabeth was certainly worth all the fuss and attention. Wasn't she beautiful! Perhaps Susanna dismissed physical beauty too lightly. There was a clear advantage to a woman's being so radiant. Still Susanna could not imagine herself as a bride. No, not she; not in the middle of all this hoopla. Susanna stood apart from the racket, on the third step up the staircase, to watch from afar.

Anne came bouncing down the stairs. It never ceased to amaze Susanna that she and Anne and Elizabeth, all sisters, could be so very different—Anne especially. Anne had adjusted her hair and her bodice four times so far that Susanna knew of. She now looked neither more nor less lovely than she had after the other three adjustments.

Anne paused beside her on the staircase. "Sukey, dear! You must go down and mix more with the guests."

"They look sufficiently mixed without my help."

20

"You do have an answer for everything, don't you. Very well, I'll mix you myself. There's Danny!" She waved an arm wildly. "And someone with him."

Like an obedient lap-dog Danny Foe answered the gestured summons. He had been smitten with Anne once; was he still? He wove in and out among well-wishers, dragging along a rather fair-complexioned chap, a likeable-looking fellow, and drew near the bottom of the stairs.

Anne made her voice as thick and soft as clotted cream.

"Good evening, Danny."

"Good evening, milady. May I present my fellow in letters and good chum, Sam Westley. Sam, the Anne I've mentioned more than once and her little sister, Susanna."

"So this is Anne." The young man's face, both open and appreciative, looked like the sort that would never ever permit an untruth. "You're supposed to be so good with words, Dan, but you didn't come close to describing how pretty she really is. And Susanna, is it?"

"Sukey, among the family here." Danny might as well consider himself family; he came around the manse often enough.

"Sukey. The littlest Annesley. Beautiful women so often have thistledown for brains—act proud of their beauty as if it weren't simply an accident of birth. I hope you're not like that, Sukey."

Susanna felt her mouth drop open and could do nothing to close it. By the time she thought of

21

something inane to stammer, Danny had shoved the brazen Mr. Westley off into the crowd. The two were laughing and talking with others now; Anne and Susanna stood on the staircase alone and abandoned.

The nerve of that brash young man! Susanna's ears burned hot enough to ignite her cheeks. She thought of half a dozen retorts on pridefulness she could have returned to him, now that he was off talking to John Dunton's cousin. Anne didn't seem to notice anything out of the way. She bounded on down into the crowd.

From her vantage point on the stairs Susanna could keep track of that brassy fellow as he moved about the room. Everywhere he went people ended up smiling. How could they be taken in so easily by his insolence? His face, his marvelously mobile face, puckered in a thoughtful frown one moment, then exploded into a delighted grin the next. Obviously the fellow was quite shallow; and he dared to suggest she, Susanna, had thistledown for brains!

Well, he sort of said that—in a way.

Elizabeth's voice by her ear startled her. "So what do you think of Sam?"

"He's a shallow boor in need of lessons in manners."

Elizabeth stared at her. "Whatever did he say to you? He's a ministry student at Mr. Veal's academy—and apparently one of the best. Writes broadsides and poetry good enough to put himself through the academy on the proceeds. Papa says he's very deep."

22

"That doesn't help his manners."

"Oh, he's extraordinarily honest and open; says whatever's on his mind at the moment. But I certainly wouldn't call being honest bad manners; in fact, I think that's part of his charm."

"Charm." Susanna made a noise appropriate to the occasion.

Elizabeth laughed suddenly. "You're a child, Sukey. You can't be expected yet to recognize a real man when you see one. You'll grow. And learn." And the beautiful bride floated off to greet more well-wishers.

A child, huh? Susanna was certainly old enough to recognize that this was exactly the sort of man she would *not* marry when she grew up. You could tell by the way he dressed and combed his hair that he was vain. In fact, he shared a good many undesirable qualities with John Dunton. Doubtless, that was why Elizabeth could use the word *charm*. Elizabeth was blinded to reality by love.

Perhaps Susanna would avoid romantic love altogether. She didn't want to be blinded by anything.

She lost sight of the churlish Mr. Westley. Might as well go down and mix in, as Anne had urged.

A young man she knew only as Martin stood by the buffet with a sausage in each hand. Martin, Susanna knew, was close to penniless. This was probably his supper—possibly breakfast and lunch, too.

"Susanna!" Martin waved a sausage. "I found the information on Apollinarianism for you. Forgot to bring the paper over, but I will one of these days."

"Explain it to me."

Martin paused long enough to swallow sausage. "Apollinaris was bishop of Laodicea somewhere around 350. He claimed Christ was truly a man but He didn't have human nature like we do. He had divine nature. He had a *soma* and a *psuche* but not a *pneuma*."

"Then He wouldn't be a man; not really."

Martin bobbed his head and wiped his mouth. "Exactly. That's what they said when bishops met at the Council of Constantinople. Officially condemned it as a heresy."

"Thank you, Martin." Susanna considered a moment. "I see that doesn't follow Socinian thought at all, any more than does Docetism."

From behind her a familiar voice purred. "The Socinians, Susanna, are Arians. Unitarians, essentially. They deny the total deity of Christ, claiming He's a created being inferior to the Father. That He lacks the complete God-nature of the Father." Sam Westley reached around her for a sausage.

Susanna put as much of the north wind into her voice as she could. "Thank you, Mr. Westley, for explaining Socinianism to me."

Martin giggled. "You missed the beat, Sammy. She is one."

The eyes in that pliant face opened wide as serving platters. "Reverend Annesley's daughter?

24

A Socinian? And here I heard that all his girls were smart."

Susanna's ears and cheeks caught fire again. "Mr. Westley, you suffer the same problem of self as do so many of these dissenter students. You think you're the only one who can correctly interpret Scripture. That, you see, is what's so wrong with the whole dissenting movement—a different interpretation for every person in it."

Martin talked with his mouthful. "I might add, Sammy, she went back to the Anglican church. She's not in her father's dissenting congregation anymore."

Susanna expected some sort of shock to register on Sam Westley's face; it was the response dissenters usually made. But no. His face softened, almost smiled. He had the look of a small boy receiving some beautiful new toy.

Mr. Westley abandoned the buffet (that in itself was probably some sort of accolade to her company), took her by the hand, and led her across the room.

He backed her into a corner and leaned with an elbow on the wall. "So tell me, Susanna, why the Socinians attract you." His eyes, soft and smoky, locked onto hers.

She drew herself up as tall as possible, to counter this sudden feeling of nervous discomfort. "They make sense. Nowhere in Scripture is the Trinity mentioned. It's an invention. I don't care to worship an invention. That's idolatry."

"You have the loveliest blue eyes."

25

She smiled. She had won. "So that's your answer to my argument. Perhaps you'd like to accompany me to our next society meeting. The Socinians welcome dissenters."

"Oh, that's not my answer to your argument. Arianism lost out at the Council of Nicea in 325, and it's been a loser every time it's popped up since. My answer to your argument is that the word is coined, but the truth it represents is not. Father, Son, and Holy Spirit are constantly and consistently given full deity in scores of passages—I'll bring you a list if you like—and frequently they're mentioned in the same breath, with correlative conjunctions giving them equal status. You know, I really do like your eyes."

"Thank you, Mr. Westley. I look forward to receiving your list."

"Want some notes on the deity and personality of the Holy Spirit while I'm at it? Socinians have a problem with that, too. You're a lovely girl, Miss Annesley. You're going to be a stunning lady."

"Thank you, Mr. Westley. And now, if you'll excuse me—?" Warmth flooded her face and neck. She lurched forward, eager to get away. But her feet stopped and turned her around to look again at that nimble, open face. "Some information on the personhood of the Holy Spirit would be welcome also, sir, if it's not too much trouble. Good evening."

He purred "good evening" to her departing back.

She fled to—to where? She hurried out into the courtyard and kept walking smartly, all the way to the end of the yard. The sweetbriers were nearly done with their blooming now, in late August. Their hips, little green knots on the ends of the stems, would be turning red soon. The English summer, so brief and episodic, was nearly over.

She inhaled deeply, but very little of the sweetbriers' wonderful aroma was left for her nose to find. Suddenly she didn't want summer to be over. She wanted it to last forever, just the way it was right now. She didn't want it trickling through her fingers like this—like dry, loose sand.

"Oh, there you are." Elizabeth came hustling across the yard. "Why are you hiding out here? Honestly, Sukey." Elizabeth hugged Susanna's shoulders tightly. "John and I are leaving now. I wanted to say good-bye."

"You're not going away forever, you know."

"No, but I'm leaving the house forever. That's frightening, in a way. And exciting." Elizabeth pushed Susanna back to study her at arms' length. "Momma's not very strong. I was carrying a lot of the day-to-day burden. That's your task now, Sukey. Take good care of her—" Elizabeth was starting to break up "—and Papa—and—" She drew Susanna in close for another tight hug.

"I shall." Susanna was certain she should also be feeling some extreme emotion, but she didn't know what it might be. Her other brothers and sisters when they married hadn't carried on like this.

27

Elizabeth clung. "Oh, Sukey, I'm so worried about you. You get these strange ideas that you think come from studying, and then you hold onto them so stubbornly."

"Papa says you fret too much, and I agree. God honors them who honor Him, and I do so. I observe all His rules as carefully as I can. I walk in the light I see, just as Papa so often preaches. I'll live such a good life God will be proud to call me home to Him."

"That's just it. You don't—oh, I wish Papa would talk to you more about salvation by faith and the failure of salvation by works. I'll pray for your soul every day, Sukey."

"Of course." Susanna pushed free; she was finding it difficult to breathe.

"God bless you, Sukey. Good-bye."

"Good-bye, Elizabeth. God bless you."

And the bride hastened away from house to house, from home to home, from life to life.

So. Elizabeth felt that now it was Susanna's province to haggle with the fishmongers. That was more or less to be expected of Elizabeth. She was the one who fussed and worried over everyone else; not just over Susanna and her religious convictions but over this household and her own; over the whole world.

Well, Susanna did not in the least feel like taking over the reins of Elizabeth's worry-cart. This household had servants enough to function without Susanna—without Elizabeth either, for that matter—and Judith and Anne were still at home. Let them haggle. It was Susanna's province to study, to show herself approved of God unto all good works, to quote Paul in 2 Timothy—not to deal with either fishmongers or worry.

For one thing, she must read up on the Trinity, especially the personhood of the Holy Spirit. If that Mr. Westley returned at all, particularly if he brought his lists, those topics would be at the top of any discussion agenda.

Perhaps Susanna had misjudged the man, based on her first impressions. He was clearly much smarter and deeper than she had given him credit for. Why, he rattled his arguments right off cold, without really even having to think about them at length. But he was still vain. He still thought much too much of himself, as evidenced by the way he so casually brushed aside her arguments in favor of his own.

He had acknowledged at the very first that physical beauty is an accident of birth, something Susanna knew well. That didn't stop him, though, from complimenting her eyes. She smiled to herself. The man might be vain and prideful, but she did admire his taste.

3

The Definition of Love

The post horse, with hooves the size of dinner-plates, plodded by on the street out front. Susanna left off her harangue with the fishwife long enough to look up, but he went right past again. She ended up paying four farthings more for the salt cod than she really thought it was worth.

Why, oh, why had Elizabeth gone off a-marrying?

The rain, until now a quiet, innocuous little drizzle, came harder. Sharp, chilly pieces of water pelted Susanna's face and shoulders. She entered the kitchen from the courtyard and dropped the hard and crusty fish on the table by the hearth. "She had eels, too, but I absolutely refused to pay what she's asking. Go down to the wharf tomorrow morning, Kate; there should be some good buys there, judging from what she was peddling."

The cook mumbled something noncommittal, glanced askance at the cod, and resumed scraping turnips.

Susanna continued down the long, hollow hall she knew so well. The door to Papa's study was closed. He didn't want to be disturbed. Silence upstairs. Mama, abed again, must be sleeping.

And nothing by the post.

She yearned for a letter. Edward Veal's academy had closed down, and some claimed that Sam Westley's sarcastic writing against the established church had hastened its closure. Susanna knew better. Mr. Veal himself had paid Sam well to write those broadsides. If it were anyone's fault, the fault lay squarely on Mr. Veal's doorstep.

Now Sam was attending Stoke Newington Dissenting Academy. It must be wonderful to pack your extra clothes in a bag, kiss your parents on the forehead, and go trooping off to school. School —nothing to do but learn and study, study and learn.

School was for boys, not for girls. No, girls need not even know how to read simple English, let alone Greek or Hebrew. Girls haggled with fishmongers and tried to choose decent husbands and birthed babies. Susanna would not let herself fall into a trap of blaming God for all that; after all, she had read the book of Job in Greek, Hebrew, and English and understood God's impatience with complainers. But someone was to blame. It wasn't fair.

She got three steps up the stairs before a rap at the door stopped her. She was tempted to just keep going on up to her beloved musty old books. Let someone else take care of it. But her father's policy, even back in the days when there were far more servants in the house, had always been to answer every knock personally. She went back down the three steps and opened the door.

Samuel Westley stood bedraggled on the doorstep like an abandoned puppy. Rivulets of rain trickled past his ears and dribbled in under the neck of his cape. He smiled wanly. "It's wet out."

"I should say." With eager swiftness she saw him to the salon, took his cloak, and bolted the length of the hall to order of Kate hot tea and cakes. Oh, yes—and a towel!

She paused outside the salon to collect herself and pat her hair. Then she stepped into the room to entertain her guest.

Sam smiled nervously. This wasn't at all like him. He was always so open and spontaneous.

Susanna smiled nervously. This wasn't at all like her. She was always in command of the situation.

"You're chilled." She broke the stumbling silence. "Let's retire to the kitchen. It's much warmer there."

"Good. Yes. Sure." He followed her down the hall, her heels clicking and his boots making gentle squishing noises.

"Please be seated." She waved an arm around the room at large.

With a relieved-sounding sigh he flopped down on the hearth stones as close to the fire as he could safely get.

Susanna pulled up her little stool and settled upon it near his elbow. She hadn't sat on her little stool in many years. She felt young again, child-sized, even though she lapped over the tiny wooden perch on all sides.

"So how is Stoke Newington?" A good hostess puts the guest at ease with a few harmless introductory questions.

"I don't know. Has your mother ever had many disappointments? Not just children dying, though I know that's sad enough. I mean—later disappointments."

"When my sister Sarah ran off and married Thomas Dangerfield. Tom was a spy; an informant for the High Church against dissenters. Caused no end of trouble and cost. Then for her to—and then there was me. I, I mean. Going back to the High Church after the shabby way it treated my father."

Susanna watched the color come back by degrees to his face as the fire warmed him. She felt a sudden yearning to wrap her arms around him and kiss the troubled tenseness out of his eyes. She would never actually do such a thing, of course—it would hardly be proper.

Sam leaned back against the bricks. "Shabby. Yes. My mother blames the established church for my father's early death at forty-two. Says it broke his heart." Sam looked at Susanna with eyes all forlorn. "She's probably right."

"I don't understand. Are you about to ask me to leave the church and return to the dissenting movement?"

34

"No!" It burst out of him. He sighed again. Such heavy, world-weighted sighs. "I'm supposed to be the word-weaver, the charmer of the printed page, the poet. And I am—until I get around you, and then my wits all fly away on the wind. I knew when I came here that everything I said would come out wrong."

She yearned more than ever to do something or say something to make it all fine for him. The youngest child in a family never gets to comfort and snuggle little brothers and sisters, and she wanted that. But she could think of nothing to do that wouldn't be misconstrued. So she did nothing.

"No, I'm not asking you to quit the church. Just the opposite." His voice had settled again to its usual melodic lilt. "You see, I'm not at the dissenting academy at Newington Green anymore. I'm enrolled at Exeter."

"Oxford! That's splendid!" She frowned. "A dissenter in school at Oxford?"

"No."

She hesitated a moment as her mind arranged all this. Here was one of the nicest things about Sam Westley. He didn't feel the need to spell everything out, as if she were a five-year-old. "I see," she said quietly. "The reason you feel so badly today is that you've sorely disappointed your mother by returning to the High Church. I understand your sadness, having seen my father's face when I turned my back on the dissenters. Doing it openly and honestly doesn't make it any easier."

Blue eyes are supposed to be cold. His were warm—warm and soft and luminous with affection. "I so fervently hoped you'd understand. And it's clear you truly do. Maybe that's why I—" He licked his lips. "Rather than sully my father's name, I'm altering mine to Wesley. Took out the *t*."

"Samuel Wesley. It pronounces nearly the same." Now how should she phrase this next question? "What, er—have you any plans? Following your education, that is."

"Yes. A theology degree. Ordination. Procure a living somewhere as a rector. My brother Matthew's studying medicine, and Mother's far too poor to help either of us financially. But once Matt and I are established, we'll be able to provide nicely for her." His voice dropped to a timid mumble. "And get married, of course."

"Of course."

Silence.

Why was her mind bumbling like this? Her stool was so small her knees poked up close to her chin. She folded her arms across them as a chinrest. "I enjoy your letters immensely. Anticipation has taught me the sound of the post horse apart from all other horses. Thank you for taking the time."

"Thank you for being so faithful about writing back. Your letters cheer me when the world gets heavy."

Kate served tea and biscuits in the thick silence. Samuel commented on the weather, but a moment later Susanna couldn't remember what he

36

had said. She commented upon the season in general. They sipped and nibbled in further silence.

Eventually Samuel gave her his address. She wished him well at Oxford. They stood about awhile fumbling for words. He studied her with those marvelous eyes and for some reason turned red briefly. Susanna was fairly certain it couldn't be the warmth in the kitchen; it wasn't that hot in here.

With much hesitation he took his leave. She draped his cloak across his shoulders; it had only partly dried. He stood about shuffling from foot to foot. He took her hand and kissed it, a gesture she had seen him use many times with women of all ages. He clung to her hand a few moments, and then he was gone.

She closed the great oaken door and leaned against it. She loved receiving letters from him. She loved his visits, which had grown less frequent lately and thus more precious for their scarcity. Why was this particular visit so unsettling?

It must have been his news that made him so uncomfortable. On the other hand that should have put Susanna, at least, at ease, for she so often felt lonely as the only Anglican in a houseful of prominent dissenters. That Sam should make the same decision healed her loneliness and persistent doubts, her constant nagging worry that she had somehow erred in her decision and thus displeased God. Above all she dreaded to displease God and invite His wrath and indignation. She must keep herself a model Christian, a person God would be proud to receive into heaven one day.

With Samuel gone back out into the rain and cold, Susanna was back to listening for the post. Southwark, that thriving, ribald, city-outside-the-city south of the Thames, had seemed an exciting place to live at one time. Now, as time stretched from days to months to years, Southwark lost its savor.

Her mother, never in good health, died quietly. A part of her beloved Papa died then also, and he spent more time than ever behind his study door. Ministerial students didn't come around as often. And because Papa felt such a strong responsibility toward them, family finances dwindled as he helped first this one, then that. One by one the servants were released, "for economic reasons." The sorry, echoing halls of Spital Yard turned cold and indifferent.

Susanna busied herself with studies, ran the household, and thought about Sam. Smart Sam. Brilliant Samuel Wesley. In some ways he was vain and full of self, just like Elizabeth's John. But there was more to him, a depth, a cleverness. He grasped things quickly. She admired that, for it was one of her own strongest traits. Best of all, Sammy accepted that she, too, had a proper head on her shoulders—not one filled with thistledown.

The year Susanna turned nineteen Sammy received his degree and became a church deacon. She was nearly as proud as if she herself had earned a degree. She understood the work involved, for Sam had no one's money but his own to put himself through. A month after her twentieth birthday he was ordained a priest. Father Samuel.

Today, Susanna giggled as she made up her bed. Father Samuel indeed. Somehow she couldn't picture Sam as anything but the witty, outgoing student who left nothing but smiles and chuckles in his wake.

She stopped in the middle of the floor. Of all the jesting, of all those times when Sam seemed to say whatever popped into his head at the moment, Susanna could not remember his ever revealing anything about himself. What did Sam Wesley feel inside? What did he think about personally? Oh, he'd talk for hours on theology and philosophy and the structure of poetry—abstract, intellectual things. But feelings? Never.

Wasn't this curious! The effervescent man who expressed himself so candidly about others could not bear to let others see the real Sam Wesley.

She crossed to her table and picked up her comb. She had arranged her hair this morning, but it was loose on the left side. So. She knew all about Sam Wesley's theology, but she knew not a single tidbit about his personal feelings. What could she deduce? He fancied her well enough; that much was obvious. On his rare visits to London he spent most of his time with his mother, and rightly so. Even so, he usually managed brief stops at Spital Yard as well. But how *much* did he like her?

He was as sensitive regarding the feelings of others as was any man. Observe how much he regretted hurting his mother when he switched churches. Even Susanna had not felt that kind of regret, although she weighed her parents' feelings carefully when she made her decision. Of course, she had been only a child back then.

She was certainly no spring chicken anymore. With her twentieth birthday behind her she had nearly passed marrying age. There were girls as old as she with three or four children already.

For that matter, how young was Sam? Come December he'd be twenty-seven. Aging Father Samuel. If he had such trouble expressing his inner feelings in words, would he also have trouble expressing love?

She paused in her doorway for a last look around. Her room was in order. She adjusted slightly her fashionable French lace collar, tugging at it so that it lay perfectly straight down her shoulders. All in order. Time to go downstairs and proceed with the rest of the day. She left her neat room behind.

Why was she worried about Samuel Wesley's propensity for love? Just because he came around and she enjoyed his company did not mean definitely and without a doubt that he would ever marry her. The fact that she had discouraged all other potential suitors did not necessarily mean Sam was the only one for her, either. Of course, he was the only one she thought about, and she thought about him often. Sometimes thoughts of him got in the way of loftier thoughts she ought to be thinking. And she did enjoy his letters. Was she in love? She wasn't certain.

Love. Why couldn't someone explain what you're supposed to feel like, exactly, if you are in love? Then she would know whether this was the real thing or not. The indefinable things of life are so frustrating. She much preferred definition, clarity, order.

Had Papa risen? Apparently—the door to his study was closed. She was halfway to the kitchen when someone rapped at the great front door. It was too early for the post. She reversed herself and took her time answering. If this was that overpriced tinker who kept coming by—

Sam stood on the stoop, resplendent in all the fine garb of the priesthood. And from inside all that fine garb glowed the childlike grin of a self-conscious little boy.

"Oh, my," Susanna purred. "Don't you dazzle the mind and eye! Do come in, Father Samuel."

"Thank you, Mistress Annesley." He entered amid the soft rustle of fresh new Lincolnshire wool.

She took his heavy, ankle-length black cloak and his flatbrimmed hat. She ushered him into the salon and stood there a moment to admire the brand new priest. Despite the boyish face he struck quite an imposing figure. "You do look the part, Father Wesley. Am I to address you henceforth as Father exclusively, or might I use less formal epithets on occasion—Papa Sammy, perhaps?"

"Now here's a side of you I never suspected—a tease."

Susanna recalled momentarily her speculations of just a few minutes ago. "There are many sides of you I can't suspect, for you never let them out where one can see them."

His cheeks turned pink. He laughed suddenly and walked off to study the carved oaken table in the corner. "I do have a bit of trouble with that, and it frequently causes me vexation." He turned around and looked at her long and admiringly. "Do you realize how very beautiful you are?"

"Your first words warned me against the pitfall of vanity."

"That was before I knew you. Before I learned you are proud but not vain."

"Proud! Really!"

"Yes, really, and rightfully so." He came back across the room to her, took her hands in his. "You're proud of your intellectual accomplishments, and no woman alive has accomplished more. Most Oxford men would envy your knowledge and skill with languages. You're proud of your upright life. You keep the commandments of God as does no one else I know. You're proud that few men are your match and none is your better."

"Do you realize what you just did? We began talking about you, and you switched it around to talking about me. You always do that. Not this time, though. Today we shall talk about the new priest, Father Samuel. What does he feel inside? What does he want? And I don't mean theologically."

"He wants Susanna Annesley. He feels he's waited quite long enough—seven years. Why, that's the bride price of Rachel and Leah, though Susanna's worth far more. You see, he has just been appointed a naval chaplain with a stipend of seventy pounds annually, which means at last he can support a wife and family. The penniless days at the college are finally over." Sam stopped. He took a deep breath. "And now he's dreadfully afraid that he's ruined a lovely friendship by letting this all spill out."

Susanna wanted to jump up and down like a child. She wanted to squeal and hug him, as Anne was wont to do. She could not. She envied at times those persons who could uncork their feelings and let them flow like wine. For all the fire burning in her breast, her head remained cold. "I'm delighted about your appointment! Congratulations."

"Thank you. I have ruined everything, haven't I? I can tell. Every time I try to explain how I feel about you, everything goes all a-bumble. I've wanted to for years and didn't because I just knew this very thing would happen."

He would have let his hands fall away, but she held onto them. "I have just as much difficulty expressing myself in some ways. I understand. And you've ruined nothing. Susanna Annesley would be proud to be a part of Samuel Wesley's life, whether she always shows it or not."

No one had warned Susanna Annesley that she was not just a scholar and a linguist or the girl of the house haggling with fishmongers. A woman of fire burned beneath the ice, a woman whose nature she had never guessed. She understood at a stroke how Jacob could toil fourteen years for the woman he loved. She still could not define the

43

word *love*, but she knew from that moment forward that she would toil a lifetime for this man Sam Wesley.

4

An Accident of Birth

Susanna raised her head from the pillow. It was
dawn, or nearly so. She poked the comfortably
slumbering man beside her. "Time to get up,
Sam."

"Bmph."

"Sam?" She jabbed.

"Another few minutes."

"No. Up now." She let her sharp voice do the
jabbing.

She perched on the edge of the bed. For a
long, ugly moment her stomach threatened to turn
over. The air was clammy in their tiny flat; how
she hated to leave the warm covers for cold air and
cold clothing.

"Sukey, beloved, why must we rise at the
same hour each day, eat meals at the same time,
share prayer and devotions at the same moment
each day? Gets a bit monotonous, you know.
What if I should feel like being pious, say, two

hours after the appointed time? Or an hour before?"

"A regular and orderly day provides that nothing will be neglected. You might well feel more pious later, but keeping to a strict order ensures that you'll be pious, whether you feel like it at the moment or not. One must never trust whim and feeling."

"You don't trust your feelings of love toward your brand new husband?"

She twisted to look at him. "You are debating in order to forestall rising, and for that purpose any topic will serve. Up."

Susanna slipped into her shoes. These soft cotton shoes were much colder than the leather slippers she was accustomed to. She must remember, next visit to Spital Yard, to bring her other shoes. She gave her wool shawl an extra wrap around her shoulders and swung the cold porridge pot in over the fire.

Sam grabbed a handful of kindling and set about reviving the fire banked last night. "You measure our hours, but must you measure the porridge? I think just once I would like to eat as much as I can hold."

"Exactly what the children of Israel said in the book of Numbers, just before God sent quails and made them all sick. The Lord provides all you need."

"True." Sam blew gently; a wisp of orange flickered and flared. He stared a bit at the seductive little flames. "I wonder if I did right to resign that ship chaplaincy. Seventy pounds was more than twice what I'm making now as a curate. Thirty pounds a year. Why, there was a day when your father's household consumed thirty pounds in a month."

"Had you kept the chaplaincy you would have been out sailing the seven seas, and I would still be haggling for eels in my father's house. I much prefer that we be together in our own household, and that couldn't happen with a ship's chaplaincy."

Sam went about his daily toilet as Susanna made up the bed. She paused by the window—her tiny, only window in this small flat. It looked out upon the wall of the building beside. Into the dank alleyway between the two buildings she dumped the chamber pot, as she did every morning.

The fire was going well now, and Sam had dropped the porridge pot lower. Susanna gave it a stir and brought out porringers and spoons. The dishes were that nice pottery made in Chelsea. The spoons, from Sheffield, had been purchased in a quaint shop on the bridge. Susanna had added much to their humble little flat here—paintings, rugs, serving pieces from among her possessions at Spital Yard. Had she married as penniless as most girls, she could never have contributed these extra pretties that added so much to the cramped and musty little rooms. Her existence and Sam's would be much more drab without these lovely touches of a finer way of life.

The water should be hot enough by now for tea. She prepared the teapot as Sam scraped away the last vestiges of his whiskers. They sat at table just as the rising sun set the forlorn little window to glowing.

Sam asked God's grace upon William and Mary and God's oversight in these present difficulties with France. He brought the whole church and its clergy to the Lord's attention. He remembered his little curacy here in a shabby corner of south London. Then he blessed the porridge and the tea.

Susanna lifted her spoon and put it down again. "There, Sam, you see? Ask and ye shall receive. I don't feel up to porridge this morning. You may have my portion as well as your own. Perhaps that will fill you as far as you will hold."

He frowned. "Are you sick?"

"Not really. Just a bit tippy inside. I feel well enough."

After breakfast they entered into daily devotions, which Susanna recognized as a rehearsal for his sermon come Sunday. He left a-visiting then— a thing he did often and well—and she brought out her musty old books for her own two hours of study.

Susanna loved these quiet hours. At Spital Yard she had indulged herself with endless hours of private study, exploring both larger questions and occasional curiosities, and she learned as much from the casual as from the formal.

A hand rapped so softly at the door Susanna was not quite certain at first that it had happened. The knock came again. She put her book aside and opened the door.

There stood a girl of perhaps fourteen or fifteen—sixteen at the very most—and obviously

48

pregnant. "Forgive me intruding, mum; might I have a moment with you?"

"Come in."

The child-woman took two steps into the room and stopped. Her eyes drifted from the flowered rug with its elaborate Greek key border to the small, delicate painting by Poussin on the far wall.

Susanna broke the silence. "Poussin was French and papist, but his work is very well regarded. And his subjects were frequently scriptural. My sister found that at a little open-air fair near Bishopsgate."

"Ye were wealthy afore ye married, I can tell."

"Reasonably so, yes. And wealthy now, for I have a good man. Please be seated."

"Thank you, mum." The girl perched herself nervously on the edge of a kitchen bench. "Would that I 'ad a good man."

"You have a man, obviously. Not a good one?"

The girl studied the dingy gray floorboards, but she didn't blush. "I've 'ad many men, mum, but none now. None of them wants a girl this big, y'ken? No man and no income; not lately. Not till this baby's born will I be attracting men again."

"I'll make tea." Susanna busied herself in the silence with pot and water and crushed tea leaves, buying herself some time to think this through. She knew about prostitutes from afar, but never had she actually—er—talked to one. And this girl appeared to feel no shame, no remorse, no idea that she might be offending either God or man.

"What I come for, mum; I didn't know where else to ask. Sure not the curate. 'E's a man. Felt better talking to a lady."

"About what?"

"M' soul. I ache for religion, least I think I do, but ken not where to find it. I'm not the sort as is welcome in church."

The tea was ready enough. Susanna poured.

The girl's eyes grew as big as the teacups. "Y've fine tea service, mum. Truly elegant. I never drunk tea from elegant cups before. This is a—a treat. Thank you, mum." And in the pools of cold hopelessness that were her eyes, a warm spark flickered.

Susanna sat down across from her. "I am Mrs. Wesley. What's your name?"

"Molly. No last name. M' mother wasn't married at the time."

"You seek religion. What do you feel is religion?"

"God, mum. Church. Worshiping God."

"Permit me to read to you from Scripture." Susanna placed her Bible on the table beside her teacup. She broke it open to St. John's gospel. "These are the words of Jesus talking to His disciples just before His passion—that is, before His death and resurrection. Chapter fifteen, verse ten. 'If ye keep my commandments, ye shall abide in my love; even as I have kept my Father's commandments, and abide in his love.' And over here in James; one of my very favorites, St. James. So practical. Here, end of chapter one. 'Pure religion and undefiled before God and the Father is this,

To visit the fatherless and widows in their affliction, and to keep himself unspotted from the world.' "

"I can't keep myself unspotted. I'm spotted."

"But you needn't remain that way. God forgives transgression. He can cleanse you, according to Scripture. But you must obey Him, and fornication and adultery are contrary to His commandments."

"No. You don't understand because you're 'ighborn. I was born spotted. I'll always be spotted, because I 'aven't no other way to be. This is all I know." Her voice fell. "It's what I am."

"I must think about this. I've never encountered this sort of problem before. I cannot believe that God would condemn you to such an existence with no way out. St. Paul said in First Corinthians, and I believe I can quote it verbatim: 'God is faithful, who will not suffer you to be tempted above that ye are able; but will, with the temptation, also make a way to escape, that ye may be able to bear it.' From that we may assume there is hope for you. A way to escape."

"I d'know." Molly frowned. "Tis a living, mum, same's any other."

"No, not the same as any other. The same as the thief's, who steals contrary to God's commandments. Or the usurer at the bank, who is just as hideous a sinner as the thief, for all his rich garments. It's not a living that pleases God. You seek religion. To please God is the highest form of religion."

"I ken what ye're saying. But I can't. I just can't." And those bottomless eyes drifted down to study her teacup.

Susanna laid her hand on Molly's. "And I don't know how to help you. I'm sorry."

Molly gazed at the hand on hers. The huge eyes brimmed up and spilled over. "'Tis the first time in m' life anyone's took the trouble to touch me gentle like that. A caring touch." She laid her other hand on top of the pile. "Mum, I'll do m' best. I just don't know 'ow to go 'bout it."

"Well, let's see." With three hands there already, Susanna added her last contribution to the stack. "Down at the wharves each dawn the fish-wives buy from the catch, then carry fish uptown to peddle house to house. No one to whom you'd sell fish cares what condition your belly's in. But you must be prepared to haggle and argue well. Perhaps something like that."

"I 'adn't thought of that sort of thing."

"And as to church. Attend regularly. Listen and learn. Make your confession and from thenceforth determine to do rightly. And after the baby's born, come to the curate to be churched."

"Churched?"

"The Thanksgiving of Women after Childbirth. It's called the churching of women. A service performed outside the service of worship, so you needn't feel uncomfortable about appearing before a congregation. It's done privately at the rail."

"Do ye think the others'll object to me being there?"

52

"If any gives you grief, send that person to me."

Molly's cheeks still glistened, but her eyes were alight at last. "Oh, mum, I do want to please God!" Her hands squeezed Susanna's. "And now, mum, I best be going. I do appreciate your time. And 'twas a lovely tea."

The girl rose. Susanna saw her to the door, gave her hands one final squeeze, and watched as Molly walked down the long, dark hall.

She closed the door and leaned against it a moment. Should she tell Sam about this unusual episode? She had no desire or reason to hold anything back from him. On the other hand, he might not understand. A church leader ought not be expected to be associated with sinners of that stripe.

Besides, in a way Susanna had just performed a ministry here, a ministry beyond her husband's scope. But ministry is a man's prerogative. Also, a decent and upstanding household must never feel the footfalls of a lady of non-virtue. Such a thing was not tolerated in polite circles. A woman, even a household member, might be a courtesan and adulteress, but she was still a giant step above the lowly harlot. No, Susanna had best keep all this to herself.

A timid knock startled her. She opened the door.

"Mum? Sorry to bother ye again. But I've friends in the same fix as me. Mought I tell 'em they can talk to ye as well?"

"Of course."

Molly burbled, "Thank you, mum!" effusively and hurried off. Susanna marveled at the change in the girl's demeanor; she carried her head higher now and walked smartly.

That settled it. If more of these girls would be coming around, this thing might become a full-blown ministry, with no other label possible for it. Susanna very definitely ought not mention the matter to anyone, Sam included.

She returned to her books, but her mind refused to stay amid their pages. She had known for as long as she could remember that physical beauty was an accident of birth; a chance occurrence blessing some women more than others. But here was another accident of birth she had never considered. What if she had been born to an unwed girl in the filth of London, instead of in the secure household of a respected religious leader?

No opportunities, no expectations. No way to learn God's will, much less to study and find ways to please Him. No way to prepare oneself for entry into heaven. That girl, five years younger than Susanna, was already an accomplished lady of the night and said she knew no other life.

An accident of birth.

When Sam returned for lunch Susanna was still pondering the ramifications of chance.

Her bridegroom kissed her warmly and gave her an extra hug.

"How's the tippy feeling?"

"Gone now, thank you." She clung to him, buried her head in his shoulder. "Elizabeth gave me a list of symptoms which signal pregnancy, and

I display several of them. I suspect that may be the case here."

He wrapped his arms around her. His boyish grin turned the dreary little flat into sun-washed Kensington Garden. "Baby Sukey! And if it's a man-child, what shall we name it?"

"With my father, my brother, and my husband all named Samuel, I have little choice; I'll call him Eleazar."

He laughed roundly and delightedly and hugged her still closer. "Lunch can wait." He tipped her face up into one of his eternal, enveloping kisses that made the world with all its weightiness tiptoe away.

All but one worldly weight. If Baby Sukey or Baby Sammy were indeed on the way—and that seemed likely—the child would be born here, in the depths of London. Not Spital Yard or a quiet village or some other wholesome place. Susanna Annesley Wesley's child would be cast among the Mollys and the men who paid the Mollys. Her child would be a part of a way of life neither she nor God could countenance.

She had so glibly quoted that passage about temptation to a girl who suffered an unfortunate accident of birth. Now she must teach that passage to a son or daughter who would walk in the midst of cruel temptation from birth on.

Rarely was Susanna Wesley ever frightened by anything life had offered her.

She was frightened now.

5

Little Sammy

Susanna clenched her hands and swallowed her scream, forcing the energy down instead of up and out.

"Good girl, Sukey! One more!"

Raging, howling pain twisted her body from the inside out. Somewhere in the haze a baby choked, sputtered, and began to cry. It was the urgent, demanding, lusty squall of a healthy newborn.

"One more, Sukey, then it's all over." The midwife's round, jolly face swam in the haze overhead. "You are the mother of a healthy son. God's blessing on the boy and on his life in service."

"Amen." Susanna lay quiet, her eyes closed, and spent some time doing nothing but breathe. She had memorized a scripture for this occasion, and now she was having trouble recalling it. *A woman when she is in travail hath sorrow, because her hour is come: but as soon as she is delivered of the child, she remembereth no more the anguish, for joy that a man is born into the world.* John 16—16—16 something.

It was true, as all Scripture is true. Already, her ordeal not even over completely, she could not clearly remember those last trying hours. Perhaps it was as well that the memory of birth pain faded quickly; this would likely not be her only experience.

"That's fine, Sukey. I'm amazed how well you've done, and this your first baby. You're very strong; I don't mean just your body, but your mind. Would that all the girls I serve were so determined to do well."

The midwife laid a tiny wrapped bundle in the crook of Susanna's arm. With two fingers Susanna pushed aside the wrapping for a better look. A minuscule, wrinkled red face pinched together in anger.

Susanna laughed. "Already he has that wonderfully mobile face like his father's. Constantly shifting, constantly telling you what's going on inside. I don't think he likes being born."

The midwife hooted. "See how warm and comfortable he was! Would you?"

Joy that a man is born into the world. Joy soothed Susanna's whole body, from the inside out. Sam had never said so, but Susanna could tell that deep inside he was hoping for a boy. Samuel Wesley I and Samuel Wesley II. Perfect. Thank You, Lord!

58

And look! Here on Samuel II's neck was a tiny birthmark, a mark just like a mulberry—mulberries, her favorite fruit.

The midwife and her girl jostled Susanna about, freshening her bed. Susanna lay relaxed and let them do with her as they would. She had worked hard. She was ready to rest.

The midwife fluffed Susanna's pillow. "You're decent again. Shall I send in your man?"

"Please. He'll be so happy it's a son."

The midwife smiled. "You're a lucky woman. So many girls around here don't have no man for to be proud of the child."

Accident of birth. That thought, pushed to the back of her mind for months, returned full force to ravel the edges of her joy. A man was born into the world. But what manner of world was this? Was the joy warranted?

Sam came bounding in with his usual enthusiasm. He even hugged the midwife in the doorway.

The woman squirmed and giggled. "Mistress Sukey, I'll return in a few hours. This being your first, I can give ye some lessons and instructions. You rest now, hear?" And she bustled out, her stolid, silent girl plodding in her wake.

Sam kissed Susanna tenderly. Then, with the caution of a man who had never done such a thing before, he lifted the bundle from her arm. The look on his face was wonderful, radiant.

Sam Second, born in mid-February, grew strong as winter waned. With spring came the linnets and robin redbreasts, the squill and primroses, and trouble in the church.

Well, it wasn't trouble exactly. Most people appreciated Sam's powerful preaching and his conscientious attitude. A few felt pricked and blistered by that very same powerful preaching, for wealth and status had hardened their consciences. And nearly every Sunday a few girls of Susanna's silent ministry would slip into the back to hear the Word of God. They never caused problems or friction. Some of the wealthy would have done well to listen with the humble hearts those girls brought to the services!

This first rare Sunday of June Susanna thought about a passage in Luke as she awaited the beginning of service. She laid Sam Second against her shoulder momentarily as she found the place, to refresh her memory. Here it was, Luke 18, where the proud rich Pharisee and the humble rich publican each sought God's blessing—and only the humble received it. She might mention that to Sam as a possible sermon topic.

Talk about humble and proud! The rector came walking in, with an obviously well-positioned man accompanying him. Although the rector was Sam's overseer in the church, as far as Susanna could remember the man had never heard him preach. Had wealthy and discontented parishioners summoned the rector with an eye to overthrowing Sam? Ah, well, the Lord's will be done here. Susanna turned it over to God and watched with idle interest the highborn fellow beside the churchman.

Sam's voice, strong and melodious, opened with the Lord's Prayer and the collect of the day. He went through the Decalogue as he did each first Sunday. Kyrie, epistle, gospel, creed—it all flowed so comfortably. Sam published banns for two couples and made a few other housekeeping announcements. In his bidding prayer he mentioned a Molly. It startled Susanna, though there were many Mollys in the congregation. But might it be she? That one?

And now, here came the sermon. And oh, my, didn't he blister the ears of the haughty and the supercilious this morning! If the rector was going to strip Sam of his curacy, it might as well be for thunder and lightning truly spoken from the Word of God. Susanna, never cool toward Sam's calling, loved him more than ever.

Communion, with all its orderly and sacred parts, proceeded apace. Susanna recited by rote as she kept a discreet eye on the rector and his companion. The man piqued her curiosity. When her turn at the rail came, Sam paused to bless his son, as always. If Sam felt at all uncomfortable or put off by the lofty visitors, he showed no sign.

Gloria, blessing, and the restless congregation poured out the door into a day of welcome spring sunshine. Susanna worked her way to the front door to stand beside Sam. All the older ladies stopped to chuck little Sammy under the chin.

The rector wedged himself in beside Sam and greeted people who might not even know who was greeting them. Sam's opposers knew. Susanna didn't know his name, but this fellow in the threadbare wool cloak was one of the most vocal of them.

He tilted his long aquiline nose toward the rector. "So what think ye, sir, of our curate?"

"Splendid message, smooth performance of the office. John?"

"I agree." It was the first the august gentleman had spoken. "I'm a sinner, as much so as any man, but I know the truth when I hear it. I wish all the church's ministers were as anointed."

The long sharp nose somehow seemed to get a bit smaller. The man mumbled something like "My sentiments exactly," though it didn't really sound that way, and sent himself one-foot-before-the-other out the door.

The rector watched him go a moment and turned to Sam. "We'd best be leaving ourselves, eh, John? Good job today, Wesley. I've heard about you; glad to get to hear you in person. My companion here, John Sheffield, Marquis of Normanby."

Sam didn't miss a beat. "Most honored. My wife, Susanna, formerly Annesley, and our son Samuel."

They exchanged pleasantries a moment, but the greater part of Susanna's mind was working on the placement of marquis in the mysterious hierarchy of British nobility; between duke and earl, she believed. And then the distinguished guests were on their way.

The river of worshipers slowed to a trickle, eventually to dry up altogether. Sam waited until the deacons had closed down and then joined Susanna for the short walk home.

Spital Fields was not one of the best parts of London, but June was certainly one of the best times of year. The warm, damp, full-blown smell of June gave one a heady sense of pleasure, of anticipation. Equally heady was the joy Susanna took in Sam's triumph. His troubles were surely not settled; in fact they almost certainly would grow rapidly in pace with summer; but for the moment she felt good. Not only had the rector supported him, but the marquis, whoever he was, also seemed well enough pleased.

The giddy joy didn't last long, of course. Susanna knew it wouldn't, though Sam seemed to hope it would. Sam was the dreamer, not she. Consistently, reality trimmed his dreams to smaller size, as a farmer shapes a hedge. Reality was not Sam's friend.

It was hers. She reveled in the methodical, the constant, the practical. Indeed, some of her routine was at last rubbing off on Sam. Two mornings a week he spent on sermon preparation. Another he devoted to the writing of serious poetry. (So far none of it had sold.) And two mornings a week he prepared articles and poetry for his pet project, the *Athenian Gazette.*

The *Athenian* had been John Dunton's idea, and John published it, but Sam was one of the three who supplied its content. It brought a tidy sum of money into this little home that needed money so badly. If not for the *Athenian,* they couldn't live.

Little Sam required much more time than Susanna would have guessed of a child so small, but she would not let him rob her of her daily study. If the reality of motherhood was constant busyness, she would master reality and bend it to her own iron will.

In July Sam received a letter from South Ormsby.

"South Ormsby?" Susanna peered around his shoulder at the seal. "Where is South Ormsby?"

"We shall soon find out." Sam broke the seal. "Oh, the criers and the broadsides have the news: on the first of this month, James was gathering his forces along the Boyne, in Ireland. William met him there and bested him roundly. James's losses were three times William's. So the throne is secure with William now."

Susanna muttered something noncommittal.

Sam scanned the letter as his face changed expressions twice. "A living at South Ormsby! They're offering me a living at South Ormsby. Their rector died—old age—and they're inviting me to replace him!"

"Where is South Ormsby?"

"A rector, Sukey! Not just a curate. My own parish to oversee. There's much to learn in running a small church. From there I can go to bigger livings with larger congregations. They say here they've about two hundred, all told."

"Two hundred in the church, or two hundred in the town?"

"Not clear on that point. Not clear on a couple points. But if their rector was old, they've probably not written such a letter in a long time. Out of practice, you know."

Sam the dreamer.

"Where is South Ormsby?"

"Somewhere around Lincoln, I believe."

"That's over a hundred miles north of London."

"They mention something about a hundred and fifty miles. Yes."

"How did they ever come up with your name?"

Sam looked at her with a smug, triumphant smile. "Recommended to them by their friend and mentor the Marquis of Normanby."

"And you'll accept."

"Of course. A splendid opportunity." His face clouded up like November. "Wait. You're a city girl. You've always lived here, never been in the country hamlets. Perhaps I should reconsider. You come first in my life. I couldn't bear to make you unhappy in some wooded swamp a hundred and fifty miles from true home."

"No. Don't reconsider. Accept. Station and beauty are accidents of birth, but surroundings are not. I don't want to raise Sammy here among the Mollys. Lincolnshire will be a much more wholesome place."

Sam was staring at her, befuddled. "Mollys? Accidents? What?"

"South Ormsby, wherever it is, represents opportunity for us both—you as a minister and I as a mother. Take the rectory, and the sooner the better."

65

He descended upon her with one of his engulfing kisses bespeaking unbridled enthusiasm. "I'll run down to the wharves and engage a carter."

"Lunch is at noon."

He laughed. "Isn't it always?" And away he went in pursuit of his newest dream.

Elusive, evasive will-o'-the-wisps are dreams. Susanna had known that from childhood, but Sam never quite seemed to grasp the idea.

South Ormsby was not what most people would call a dream, not by any stretch of imagination. Many miles from Lincoln, the only large town, South Ormsby perched on a rutted mud track, clung to the slippery shores of the endless, boggy moors and forests of the Lincolnshire Wolds. Around it here and there, gloomy little farmsteads huddled amid scraggly pastures. Low stone walls sometimes kept the woodlands at bay and sometimes not, for Susanna saw many a small tree sprouting on the pasture sides of the fences. Utter wildness, like a living thing, lurked in all the woods and glades to whisper accusingly in Susanna's ear, *You never should have come here; this is not your place.*

Susanna ignored the chills this remote desolation sent down her back. Fens and forests possess a pervasive, dank smell of decay all their own. Still there was no smell of filth and raw sewage here as there was in London. In the villages and hamlets she saw all manner of urchins and feebleminded and ragged elderly, the decay of being poor. But they showed none of the blank hopelessness one saw in the faces of London's poor, and Susanna saw no girl with the downcast eyes of London's Mollys.

After an eternity of winding along narrow dirt lanes that pretended to be real roads, they arrived at the rectory beside the little church. The 206 souls boasted of in the letter composed the full population of the village, and quite probably a few of the dogs had been included in the number. On their slow, dismal ride through the village Susanna counted thirty-six dwellings.

The rectory itself, a mud hut with no glass behind the shutters, probably dated from the Roman occupation. It had been cleaned and swept nicely, a credit to the goodwives of the little village. And because she had just moved from a very small flat, Susanna could fit all her furniture into this tiny room-plus-loft cottage.

The poverty and meanness stilled Sam's ebullience momentarily and turned him into a sober, long-faced penitent. Then the dream ignited again, and he was his usual self as he helped the carter tote in belongings.

Susanna sat in a corner as the house filled and the sun drifted down behind the trees. She dandled little Sammy on her knee and wondered pensively if she would ever see London again.

6

South Ormsby

Her name was Molly, too, but she bore absolutely no resemblance to the Molly who had rapped on the door of Susanna's flat in London. Well, there was perhaps one thing alike; her knock was almost as timid.

She was as wide as two London Mollys and twice as old. She sat now at Susanna's little table—her face raw and weatherworn like the Lincolnshire Wolds themselves—and sipped tea from one of those delicate little cups the other Molly had liked so well. The coarse, burly hands contrasted curiously with the fragile white pottery. Daintily she wiped her mouth on the hem of her apron.

"Thank you, Miz Wezzley, mum, for inviting me in like this. We be naught more than simple rural folk here, as ye know; don't know quite how to greet elegant city people. I mean, when they comes to live amongst us. Now the marquis, he just makes himself to home down to the pub. But that's different, of course."

"The Marquis of Normanby. I understand he has a summer home out here in South Ormsby."

"Aye, up behind the glen there. Huge place. My cousin's niece works as a chambermaid there, and my husband's brother's uncle—on his wife's side—does the gardening. Got three helpers, he does."

"Comes up often?"

"In summer, aye. Not when the roads are bad. Big house, likely quite chill in winter despite its great fireplaces." She snickered. "There's good advantage to living humble in a country croft, eh, Miz Wezzley? So warm and cozy when the wind comes howling."

"Indeed. Have you met his wife?"

"No, mum." A great block of winter ice seemed to come crashing down upon the voice and manner. Perhaps there were hard feelings there; Susanna quickly shifted topics.

"You mentioned gardening. The vegetable patches here seem to be less advanced than the ones we saw in London. Of course, that was nearly two months ago now."

"Eh, y're right. We're a bit behind London, I hear; cooler here, little later getting the good weather of spring. But we can still enjoy our mustard greens and broadbeans after yours are all gone. And our chard comes earlier. And ye see how well the cabbage is doing this year! Good hard heads; they'll store well. Less sickness in the winter when it's been a good cabbage year."

Already Susanna had heard more about gardening than she cared to know, but Molly was waxing enthusiastic on what was obviously a favorite subject—how the hamlet's general health seemed to be influenced by the kinds of vegetables grown in plenty. "Ye see, Miz Wezzley, different things grow better some years than others, it seems."

Susanna really wished the garrulous lady would leave. She felt bad and was beginning to feel worse. Her headache and her nausea, which had never really left her today, fought each other for control. Little Sam snuffled, fussed a moment, and began to wail.

"Awake already. His naps get shorter and shorter." Susanna started to lurch to her feet, but a brawny hand gripped her arm.

"Ye sit now, Miz Wezzley. I haven't bounced a baby in years, and I'd love the chance this once, if I mought." Agile as a ten-year-old, the hefty woman bounded to her feet and crossed to Sammy's cradle. With coos and giggles and happy faces she scooped him up and brought him to the table. "Eight months old now, I ken."

"Almost exactly. You've a good eye."

"Better'n ye know." The lady's whole face twinkled. "If I might be so bold, I'd judge y'r next one's due in spring."

Susanna wagged her head. "I didn't realize I showed yet."

"Shows early on slim and pretty girls, such as y'rself. Y're city bred, mum, and may not ken. But here in the country, everyone knows everything

71

about everyone, maybe even before they knows it themselves. Courtships and babies and who's slipping around on the sly. It's all known. 'Tis the way of it out here."

"I'm sure when I learn people's names and become more familiar with the area that I'll get to know everyone better."

Molly nodded and wiped Sammy's droolly chin with the hem of her apron. "More or less. But gossip usually ain't fitting for the ears of the preacher's wife, so you may be the last to know. How it's been in the past, anyway."

"Gossip's not fitting for anyone's ears, Molly. St. James specifically warns about the damage the tongue can do."

"Umph. I 'spect St. James never lived in South Ormsby."

Winter treats some parts of the world kindly, Susanna had heard. In tropical climes, no harsh north winds claw at one's cheeks and bring tears to the eyes. Biting cold never seeps through the window cracks or shoulders its way in under the loose thatching. But she was not in a tropical clime.

Sam really was going to have to get their place rethatched. Susanna curled up in bed with the comforters piled high and watched rainwater drip from between two loose boards in the loft. The drips missed the bed by inches.

Little Sam crawled lickety-split across the floor, like a racehorse in the homestretch. He stopped at the table, flipped to sitting but a moment, then pulled himself to standing with the table leg. He'd be walking shortly; then Susanna would really have her hands full!

Beside her in the bed, huddled against her breast, baby Sukey squirmed. Quickly Susanna offered her dinner, but the baby hardly seemed interested. A few moments of nursing and she drifted off to sleep again. So tiny. The child was so tiny. Born much too early, little Sukey. She wasn't due until April at least, and here she was already with spring not even in the air yet.

The mud-hut rectory felt even smaller now, with the last gasps of winter ravaging it, as cramped and confining as the little pantry back home in Spital Yard. No, Susanna mustn't think that. This was home now, the place where God had put her. Spital Yard was past. Gone.

Little Sam headed straight for the chamber pot, and Susanna was nowhere near quick enough to catch him in time. Saved! Big Sam came charging in the door amid a swirl of wind and cold rain. Instantly distracted, Sammy Junior rotated onto his bottom, altered direction, and crawled to Papa in that four-legged lope.

Sam shed his cloak, gathered up his son, and plumped down on the edge of the bed. "Mrs. Wickham missed church last week because her three were down with the croup and the mister's working up in Grimsby until May. Hiram Haye claims there's smallpox and typhoid both in Lincoln, but he's not heard of any closer. That little blonde girl—married the pig farmer, you remember?—finally bore her child; a boy, named William

73

for the king." He leaned over to rub Susanna's shoulder. "Feel any better?"

"No stronger. Spending most of the winter abed didn't do a thing for me."

"And how is Sukey?"

"She's so listless. Not bright, like Sam was. And very hard to keep warm. Her little hands and feet turn cold the instant I move her away from my own body warmth."

Sam's features melted further, from concern to sadness. "The Lord giveth, and the Lord taketh away. Blessed be the name of the Lord."

"And in all this Job sinned not, nor charged God foolishly." Susanna completed the thought from the book of Job.

"I've read that passage a score of times and never until now realized how strong a man Job was." Sam pushed aside the blanket and ran a huge, stocky finger down the tiny cheek. "She's so delicate. And beautiful. Like you."

Never quite full-size, never quite fully active, frail baby Sukey died. Emilia came along, though, in 1692, and made up in robustness all her sister had lacked. Twins arrived the next year, and both died. In December beloved Queen Mary died, too—of smallpox. She was only eight years older than Susanna.

When Susanna bore a baby girl in 1695 she named it Susanna and petitioned the Lord especially to spare this one. He did so.

Susanna herself was feeling stronger, too. The first Susanna had drained her, the twins even more so, both physically and emotionally. In her six years of marriage so far she had borne six children. But now, for the first time in a very long time, she could work the day through without having to lie down.

Today she leaned in her open doorway and watched five-year-old Sammy build an elaborate castle out of mud from the roadside ditch. Her pride and her sorrow, little Sammy.

Here came Papa Sam down the road, and Susanna could tell from a quarter mile away that his visitations had not gone well. A thick cloud seemed to hang above his head to cast darkness on that expressive face.

Little Sam came popping out of the ditch to greet his father. He froze in place, uncertain; he could read faces as well as anyone.

"Greet your papa later, Sammy. Go play now. Besides, you don't want to get mud all over Papa's frock."

The boy's eyes shifted from face to face a moment. Then he submerged himself again in the ditch, hauling building materials, watching every movement from a safe distance.

"I'll make you a pot of tea while you tell me what has gone wrong with your day." Susanna brought herself erect and stepped into the darkness of her home.

"What's that baker woman's name?"

"Matty Billings, or Emma Dorsett."

"Billings. That one." Sam threw his hat onto the bed and almost woke both Emilia and little Sukey. "She stopped me on the street and commented on the fact that our Samuel has never once spoken a word."

"It's common knowledge. Nothing goes unknown in this village." Little Sammy, her pride and her sorrow.

"First she asked me if he can hear."

"Of course he can hear. You speak to him and he obeys. Sharp sounds startle him."

"She decided that as well, delightful woman that she is, for much the same reasons. She tells me she even clapped her hands once when he passed her gate, just to see if he'd turn."

Susanna dropped leaves into the teapot and clapped the lid down. "If this were London I'd say it's none of her concern, but this being Ormsby, such things are apparently everyone's concern. You didn't explode again, did you?"

"Not just then. When she compared our Sam to the Holletts' idiot child, that's when I got angry."

"And you forgot all those prayers you offered God regarding your temper and caused an ugly public scene again."

"He's not an idiot!"

Baby Sukey scrunched her face. Emilia opened her eyes.

Susanna sighed. "No, Sam, he's not an idiot. Neither does he speak. Mute or talkative, he's the Lord's servant. Let the neighbors think what they wish."

Sam sat scowling at his teacup.

"Did you get another letter from John Dunton?"

He looked at her. "Now you read minds. Yes."

"I do wish you two would patch up your differences, for my sake and Elizabeth's if not for your own. You do enough squabbling with near strangers. You shouldn't be at odds with one of your best friends. It's hard on you. You're not that kind of person to take it lightly."

"The *Athenian's* folded."

"What?"

"The *Athenian Mercury*. The periodical I've been writing articles for all these years. John closed it down."

"This was supposed to be a three-man enterprise; you, John Dunton, and Richard Sault. What has Richard to say about it?"

"The letter didn't mention Richard's opinion." Sam rubbed his face and nearly tipped his tea. "John said circulation was down, and the chore was becoming burdensome. Sukey, I wrote a third of that paper every week. My poetry—sure, there was some doggerel, but there was some very good stuff, too."

"I see. And John wrote that he didn't want to edit your doggerel any more."

Sam's cheeks were getting red. They only did that when he was worried as well as angry. "This living pays fifty pounds a year."

"I know."

"There's no way we can live on fifty pounds a year; I'm already in debt more than that amount. I need the money the *Athenian* was bringing in. I mean, *we* need the money."

"The Lord feeds the ravens of the field."

"Not on fifty pounds a year, He doesn't."

"You're bordering on blasphemy."

"And I don't need a lecture on religion right now."

"You've already awakened the children. I suggest you take a long walk—down to the fens, perhaps; the wildland there seems to soothe your nerves as well as any place—until you've brought your ire under better control. I married you for better or for worse, but I would just as soon the worse not take place in my presence."

He glared at her hotly, then bolted upright, snatched his hat from the bed, and stormed out. She closed her eyes a few moments and wished the children's were still closed as well. She knew the pattern Sam's actions would take. He would huff and puff and walk and snap at people. Like a porridge taken from the fire he would simmer and wane until, like porridge, he would be cool enough to endure. In a few hours he would be back at the door, contrite and looking for his next rainbow.

Susanna gave Emilia a bit of bread for herself and one for brother and sent her out to play. She changed Sukey and was just about to feed her when someone rapped at the doorjamb.

A very nicely dressed woman stood there. The hat was correct for this season. Her lace collar lay just to the points of her shoulders. She was somewhat older than Susanna and really quite pretty. Susanna's first impression was that this might be the marquis's wife, for in the five years they had been at South Ormsby, Susanna had never once met the lady.

"Do come in, madam. Tea is made. May I serve you?"

"That's very nice of you. Thank you." The woman stepped forward. "You're Susanna Wesley, the rector's wife?"

"Yes. Am I—"

Little Sukey got tired of waiting. She tied herself in a tight knot, knees pulled up, and let go with her "Now!" wail. What should Susanna do? One does not nurse a child in front of a marchioness.

"Oh, I'm sorry to have disturbed one of the most urgent things in life." The woman smiled kindly. "If you don't care to feed the child in front of a stranger, I'll return later."

"I would enjoy your company." Susanna let Sukey howl until she had offered the lady a chair and poured tea. Then, at last, the squirming and the screaming stopped.

The woman sipped in the sudden silence a moment, as if uncertain what to say. But then, what does her ladyship say to a simple rector's wife? "I have increasingly felt the urge to come call. To—uh—talk to someone about, well, you know— Then I thought it best to wait until after your newborn was a bit bigger."

"And I, too, would have come calling, but I never quite know when you'll be at your summer place. The marquis seems to come and go at odd times."

Huge limpid eyes snapped up to look at Susanna. They drifted down to the teacup again. "Lovely cups."

"Thank you."

"Now I understand the warmth of your greeting. You seem to think I'm John Sheffield's wife."

"Your elegance suggested that."

"Thank you." Her eyes clung to Susanna's, the expression of a child who has just erred badly and hopes to avoid a beating. "But I'm the marquis's widow."

Susanna gasped. "He's died? Oh, no!"

"No, no! He's alive and well. You mean you haven't heard about me? I'm not a lady. I'm just simple rural folk, and a widow. Ask any gossip: the marquis's widow is the woman who shares his bed when his wife is back home in London."

7

A Missing Boy

Autumn bullies London harshly. She rudely washes away the warmth of summer with cold rain and clammy skies. She rarely bothers to convert the few trees to delightful colors, robs the grass of its green, then leaves no promise but a bleak and dismal winter. Lincolnshire, though, she brushes across gently.

Susanna strolled down the narrow lane near the fens, tasting and smelling and watching the rapid advance of autumn. Dry grass crackled near the stone fence. It was much too early in the evening for hedgehogs to be out. She watched a moment before glimpsing a familiar tail and face; little Sammy's cat was out prowling.

The various brown hedge sparrows had already left Lincolnshire, but the busy little blue tits with their white faces still skittered about in the trees. And the rooks were in for their autumn roosting.

Susanna's father had always referred to any black bird as a jackdaw, but Susanna had learned the differences. Rooks were smaller than ravens and larger than jackdaws. Rooks had bald gray faces to match their gray beaks. Their voices were far less annoying than ravens', and they roosted. Susanna had heard of their vast, communal autumn roosts even when she lived in the city. But now here she could watch them.

From miles around they came, by twos and tens and bunches, to settle in the old oaks by the fens. Noisy, jostling, bickering, constantly jockeying for the perfect position, they reminded her of nothing more than a giant conclave of village aldermen. Thousands of black-clad, balding, petty officials—the notion tickled her fancy.

She sat to rest a moment on a stile beside the lane. This may have been a serious mistake, taking a walk. She had been in bed ill too long; she was still too weak to walk so far. Ah, well. If she got too tired she would simply wait beside the lane. The hired girl knew which direction she had taken. The girl would tell Sam, and Sam would come looking for her eventually.

The hired girl had become a necessity, with Susanna so frequently ill. She couldn't properly manage tiny children when she was bedridden. Having grown up with a houseful of domestics to handle all the daily chores and children, she was once used to extra help. But the manse at Southwark had been a thousand times bigger than this little hovel, with a thousand times more furnishings to care for. And in London when one hired, one could pick and choose from a score of applicants. Out here in South Ormsby Susanna had almost no choice, and frankly she hadn't liked any in the whole lot. Still, this girl was better than none.

More rooks than Susanna could have imagined were flocking in now from near and far—just like troubles. Winged black shadows that couldn't simply visit occasionally and alone, they came in bunches from unexpected directions to flutter down into the naked black trees. A chill breeze shifted and rose. She had best start back.

Her hem brushed the dead weeds and picked up some burrs as she stepped out into the lane. She'd let little Sammy pluck them out. He delighted in jobs of that sort.

He was getting old enough to begin reading and ciphering. How could she teach him to read when he couldn't speak? How would she know he had learned his lessons if he didn't recite them aloud? Perhaps she should teach him to print his alphabet and write first. Would that work? It sounded inside out, but what else could she do? Sam the optimist kept saying to wait; everything would work out just fine. Susanna didn't want to wait much longer. The boy was bright and quick and ready to learn now.

With two more rest stops she finally arrived at her door. She had just added new dimensions to the meaning of "weary." A cup of hot tea, dinner, and to bed. It sounded so good.

The stew bubbled softly well to the side of the fire. Susanna had supervised its start several hours ago. Now, at its end, it smelled delicious. The maid had spread the great linen cloth over the table and set the bowls and spoons about, all ready. Susanna really ought to cut that tablecloth in half; it reached to the floor; but there might be a day when their table would be long enough to fit it. Better too big than too small. Besides, it looked more elegant than did the bare oak slab table.

Susanna glanced around. "Where's Sammy?"

The maid looked up from husking broadbeans. "Sammy? Uh— There's Emilia. And the baby's sleeping."

"I see Emilia. Where's your brother, Emilia? He's not lost, is he?"

"No." Already, at less than three, Emilia was building sentences from her endless stream of words. "The cat is lost."

"You mean Sammy went out to look for the cat?"

Emilia nodded. "We want it. Pway wiff it."

Susanna glared at the maid. "You let him wander off?"

"He didn't say nothing 'bout leaving, mum."

"Of course he didn't! Mind the baby." Susanna grabbed Emilia by the hand and walked out to the ditch. "Sammy? Saaa-meee! Clap your hands!" She listened. That north breeze was picking up; it rattled the brown leaves on the willows beyond the ditch.

"Samuel, where are you?"

She tried the back of the house. No response. With Emilia in tow she hurried to the crossing. No answer. Fears, like a roost of rooks, came flocking in to weigh down her heart.

Here came Mrs. Crittendon up the road. The stocky little widow might be crabby and short, but she was good with children.

"What's wrong, Mrs. Wesley?"

"My Samuel's wandered off to find his cat. I'm afraid he's lost."

"What kind of cat?"

"The cat's not lost. I saw it down by the fens. Little Sammy is lost."

"Ne'er mind. I remember your cat. Pretty thing. Sammy's lost, you say. The mute. I'm on my way to Hodells' right up yonder. Hodells and me, we'll pop out and look around, too. Getting chill; don't want the lad out all night." And she waddled off up the road.

Within minutes other neighbors had popped out as well. A lost child was a matter of immediate community concern just as was a juicy bit of gossip, though probably not more pressing.

"Samuel, where are you?"

Susanna had come to the end of her endurance. She plopped down on the little stool by the front door and gathered Emilia in close. The child's arms were frigid; Susanna had been dragging the poor tot about without so much as a summer-weight shawl.

Sam came boiling down the street at a dead run, and Susanna had never seen his face quite so tight and drawn. "Have they found him?"

"Not yet, that I know."

"I heard from Mayhews that he's lost, as I was coming back from the glen. Harold's talking about dragging the south side ditch tomorrow." Sam's

85

voice cracked. He glanced at Emilia and paused to compose himself. He squatted beside Susanna's stool.

"Samuel belongs to God regardless the outcome of this." It sounded so brave. Susanna dwelt on the words as they left her lips. They tasted bitter.

"I know," Sam whispered. "I know. But he's our firstborn, Sukey, and our only boy. Must God have him just yet?" He looked at Susanna, and his burning eyes bespoke fear so loudly that Emilia stared at him and cringed against her mother.

"I don't know how far this hue and cry has spread, but I can walk no farther. Perhaps if you wish to pray on your feet you can look with Hodells near the rookery. He might have gone somewhere out that way."

Sam nodded and rubbed his face. "When one of my congregation loses a child I glibly counsel him to be strong. I'll remember this next time." He hugged Susanna and broke a cardinal rule about displaying affection in public; he kissed her forehead. Then he was off again, with a boyish energy born of fear, not youth.

"Oh, Samuel, please; where are you?!"

Susanna hugged her Emilia a few minutes, then stood up.

"Come, dear, let's go inside. It's getting cold out." *Too cold for a boy not yet six years old, who has no wrap or shelter against the night.*

The stew still simmered, but the aroma had lost its savor.

"Shall I feed Emilia, mum?" The maid murmured in tones contrite, as well she should; she had let him wander off.

"Please. I'll eat later, with Sam."

The maid had opened the shutters along the fireplace wall. Susanna stood at the open window and felt the curious contrast of cold wind before and warm room behind. She offered up prayer, as one must do, for God controls all, but her prayer felt dry in her heart. That would never serve. Didn't God say, "Because you are lukewarm I shall spew you out of My mouth?" Fervent prayer avails much; dry, cold supplications were no doubt worthless.

Sam never made dry, cold supplication. He was a model of enthusiasm under any circumstance. In a way, Susanna envied his mercurial highs and lows, but not at times like these. Sam tended either to blow up or fall apart in extremity even as Susanna, neither hot nor cold, could calmly and effectively continue on.

Still, she felt frustration and fear no less keenly than he. They welled up in her now. When Sammy most needed her, her weary legs and laggard heart refused to let her seek him. Frustrating! Lincolnshire was more woods than meadows, with bogs and fens to snare the innocent and unwary. She had heard tales of grown men becoming hopelessly lost in the wilder tangles.

She sat down on the wide sill, because her legs would hold her no longer, and gazed out across the fields beyond the tiny rectory. The meadow grass lay pallid in its annual death, beaten down by rain and cattle, devoid of green.

Her fear and frustration boiled over, exploding as words. "Samuel Junior, *where are you?!*" They rolled out across the empty lea on the waning, chilly breath of autumn.

"Here I am, Mother."

Susanna felt her mouth drop open and could not close it. She wheeled so rapidly on her perch she nearly fell off.

The voice—that wonderful, plaintive, gentle child voice—came from where? The very middle of the room, it seemed. An angel? Nonsense. No angel would appear to a woman as practical and ordinary as Susanna.

The long tablecloth jiggled slightly. Weary legs forgotten, Susanna dived to the floor. Together her long, slim mother-hand and a chubby son-hand lifted the linen hem. Apprehensive blue eyes peeked out.

She scooped Samuel up, gathered him in, and together with the prodigal's father could sing, "For this my son was dead, and is alive again; he was lost, and is found."

And not just the rooks of fear and frustration, but even the rooks of her sorrow for a son who could not speak—all of them flew away.

8

A Difference of Opinion

"Mrs. Wesley, g'day." Mr. Strood the butcher stood in her open doorway with a hooded cape pulled close around his ears, his shield against the drizzle of late spring. He looked jovial enough, but Susanna knew that his satin face masked an iron core.

"G'day, Mr. Strood, and what can I do for you?"

"M'self has stopped by today, mum, strictly for y'r own convenience, that ye need not walk clear to m' shop to put a bit more down on y'r bill outstanding."

"Very thoughtful of you, sir, but I have no money here in the house. My husband carries our only purse. Thank you, though, for stopping by."

"And when might I expect payment?"

"I shall ask my husband when he returns."

Mr. Strood stepped inside and closed the door behind him. In the gloom he seemed somehow bigger, more ominous. "Mum, I do need a bit on account now."

Susanna felt the back or her neck prickle. "I keep all the commandments of God, Mr. Strood, as should you if you wish to avoid God's wrath, and I resent your inference that I would lie about the matter. There is no money in the house."

Whoever knocked at the door just then didn't wait for an answer. The door swung open.

The marquis's widow entered. "Thought that was you, Strood. G'day, Mrs. Wesley."

"Good day, and welcome. If that is all, Mr. Strood—"

"Y've got y'r uppity airs, Mrs. Wesley, for a woman so deep in debt. A maid! Ye owe every merchant in the village, and you hire a maid. Debts come first."

"You self-righteous prig!" the widow exploded. "The woman's been ill, bedridden most of the time, and here are her four little ones to be cared for. Yet you would deny her the help she needs!"

"Y've no right to criticize a decent man, you—"

Rarely did Susanna raise her voice. She screamed it out now. "Enough! Mr. Strood, you will leave now, for I have nothing for you. And if it sets your heart at ease, I dismissed the maid not long ago."

The butcher's eyes flicked from face to face. In a huff he wheeled and stomped out. The door slammed behind him.

Susanna glanced at young Sam. "Sam, will you take Emilia up to the loft to play, please?

There's a good boy. Emilia, go with your brother. I'll tend Sukey down here." She watched the tots jog up the ladder.

When the gentle widow wrapped both arms around Susanna she didn't resist. She melted against the scratchy wool cape and hugged back, rejoicing in the warm comfort of a friend who cared.

She stepped back presently. "The water's hot. Tea in a moment. Sit down near the fire here. I'm so glad you came by."

"That Strood. Owe him a farthing, and he'll dun you to the grave."

"I can see his side. The man must make his living, and he has no obligation to carry us on his back. He could be a little more polite about it, though."

"How's little Molly?"

"Sam's still convincing himself that she'll be fine with time, but I know better. She'll be crippled for life."

"I can't believe that maid could be so careless!"

"I'm surprised Mr. Strood hadn't heard that I fired her. It must be all over town."

"Oh, he heard. The tale's magnified, of course; always is. But it's still fairly accurate. Your baby Molly nearly died, and now faces life as a cripple, because of the girl's carelessness. But do you know, the girl's family still thinks you were wrong to dismiss her. 'Just a simple mistake,' they're saying."

Susanna stared at her. "I would forgive a mistake. But never carelessness." She busied herself with tea, lest her hands start shaking.

"If I may be bold, Sukey, you're looking a little better now that you're a few more months along. A bit of color in your cheeks again. Pregnancy surely does go hard with you."

Susanna smiled. "I should certainly be accustomed to it by now, this being my eighth."

The woman shook her head and changed subjects—in the wrong direction. "Heard from home lately?"

"Yes, just recently. My father's estate is finally settling. Very little left in it; he was mentor to a number of ministerial students, as you know, and was generous in their support. Which is as it should be. His estate came from his life of service to our Lord and should go the same way."

The tea was close enough to steeped. Susanna sat down and poured. "Benny says St. Paul's Cathedral is in use, although it's nowhere near done yet." She sipped her tea; the cup rattled against the saucer. She must control her hands better.

"Sukey, what else?"

"I was the last born of twenty-five, and my mother was frail. The children more or less took care of each other, because our nanny wasn't too efficient in some ways. My sister Elizabeth took me under her wing, you might say. We were very much alike, Elizabeth and I. She was special."

"Was?"

"Benny informs me Elizabeth has died. She was—she was still young."

A warm, soft hand closed over Susanna's. "I'm so sorry."

"Benny said a Puritan preached her funeral. A Timothy Rogers. That wouldn't mean much to you, but I—"

The door opened; light gushed into the room. It surely wouldn't be the butcher back; not without knocking.

Sam!

"I went calling down to the hollow, but no one was home. It's a ghastly day out, and I thought a spot of tea would b—" He stood as if pole-axed, staring at the marquis's widow.

Susanna could read his face as it melted from shocked surprise to vivid fury. She must say something before Sam's instant temper boiled over. She opened her mouth—but not in time.

Sam seized the widow's wrist, lifted her bodily from her chair, and hauled her to the door.

Susanna leaped to her feet yelling, "No, Sam!" but she was too late. Sam shoved the woman out the open door into the cold, rainy slop.

Susanna seethed with rage. She ought to hold her tongue; this was the man of the house. She would do no such thing! "How dare you treat my friend so shabbily!"

"That woman— That woman is— Not in *my* home!"

"St. James calls us to hospitality. He does not place limits upon it, and you have just violated it severely. You will go out to my friend, and you'll—"

"Don't you realize who she is? She's the—"

"The marquis's widow. Yes, I know very well who she is. What you don't seem to know is that she is a lovely, sensitive woman who yearns for close, solid friendship, as do I, and you—"

"I can't believe you, of all people, would defend an adulteress!"

"God says to keep unspotted from sin. God also says not to judge, lest we be judged. Abhor the sin and love the sinner; remember that sermon you preached not long ago? Does it apply only to men and not women?"

"She's not fit company for any but harlots! And she'll not come under my roof again. Never!"

"*She's* not fit company!" Susanna pitched her voice louder to match his. "The marquis is fit company for you, for I've seen you together often. An adulterer! The marquis attends services, but she's not allowed to. Yet he's as guilty as she. I daresay more so! He's the one with responsibility toward a wife."

"It's hardly your place to criticize either the marquis or me in this matter."

"You're saying that when a man falls he's not really fallen at all, but a fallen woman wallows in the gutter forever. That's hardly the morality of Scripture! That's hypocrisy!" Vaguely Susanna became aware of eyes watching. She glanced upward.

Up in the loft Sammy and Emilia gaped. Little Sukey cringed in the chimney corner as if lightning were about to take the house down, and baby Molly fussed in her cradle.

Sam must have bridled his fury for the children's sake, too. He looked from child to child and

94

adjusted his voice downward. He wagged a finger in her face. "You will never ever again accuse me of hypocrisy, and you will never again let that woman in this house or permit her to enter the presence of my children." And out he stormed.

Susanna watched him fill the doorway, then get smaller as he marched away. In his haste to leave he nearly bumped into Granny Sykes, standing all ears near the opened door.

So be it. If Granny Sykes wanted to spread the rector's domestic fight all over town, so be it. Amen, so be it.

No! She and Sam often disagreed on a thing, but rarely did they fight. And they never got into shouting matches with the children observing. Sam would shout; that was his way; but Granny had got the wrong idea, and now she'd be perpetuating the wrong idea, magnifying it, dwelling on each delicious little detail.

Susanna sat down at her table and leaned one elbow on it. She must calm herself, lest she bear this baby unbetimes, as she had the first Sukey and the twins. She sniffed. She sobbed aloud. She pulled her apron to her face and let it all come, torrents of sorrow flooding at once.

Why had her beloved Papa had to die alone, without her at his side? No one sent for her; indeed, no one told her he was gone until months after the fact. She mourned him deeply.

Why couldn't he have clung to enough of his estate to bring Susanna out of debt—or at least help a little? Sam served God. Surely a bit of God's money could go to paying his bills.

For that matter, why couldn't Sam hold onto even a farthing? No matter what the income, he managed to exceed it. On Fridays instead of writing "serious" poetry, why couldn't he write something that would bring a few pounds into the house? Susanna was abysmally sick of constantly scratching, of being dunned.

Why did Elizabeth have to die? She was so pretty and young and so good for John whether Susanna particularly liked John or not. Was Elizabeth's illness the reason John Dunton gave up on the *Athenian*? It didn't matter anymore. That source of income was dried up, too.

How could Sam be so hypocritically pigheaded about the marquis? And about one of Susanna's few true friends? She understood. She cared. She poured her troubles out to Susanna, and Susanna felt safe to share her troubles as well, for the woman was no bearer of tales. And now she was gone, violently evicted by an unfeeling, unreasoning man with a blind, narrow-minded view of morality and women. If Sam were to cheat, no one but Susanna would care. Were Susanna to cheat she'd be abandoned on the street in a moment. It just wasn't fair! Elizabeth's death wasn't fair, or Papa's, or the way money was distributed in this world, or the way an uncaring girl could so casually cripple a poor baby and nearly kill it—or—or—

A tiny tug jiggled her skirt. Little Sukey's huge blue eyes glowed beside her knee. The tot scrambled, and Susanna hauled; Sukey curled up tight into a warm, safe knot in Susanna's lap. A few moments later two other uncertain little children were seeking lap space.

Susanna took a deep breath and almost brought the weeping under control. "Come, children. Let's all of us take a rest. You can't all fit if I'm sitting up." With Sukey on her hip she stood up carefully and walked over to the bed. The moment she lay down, squirmy children with thumpy feet snuggled up against her. With the things that matter most packed in on all sides, she dozed.

Susanna had guessed right about the speed of gossip in this tiny hamlet. Women didn't even wait until her back was turned to start tittering, heads together. Worship services in the little church felt tense. The whole fabric of her life stretched askew and frayed at the edges.

What, of all the stories going around, did the marquis hear? When next he came out to South Ormsby he called for Sam. Sam spent hours alone with the fallen marquis, and Susanna yearned to visit again with the fallen widow. What did the men discuss? Such things were confidential between priest and parishioner; Sam never said, and Susanna hardly expected him to. Frankly, she didn't really care, either. The marquis's view of the relative morality of men and women matched Sam's, as it matched all men's, and as far as she was concerned they could all slosh down to the Wash and jump in.

Come spring though, the gossips and the tattletales became too busy to give the vicissitudes or the Wesley household their undivided attention. Molly the inveterate gardener brought fresh greens, and Susanna was deeply grateful. Was it a love offering, for Molly was a warm and open soul? Or was it a guilt offering, because she was also one of the village's prime news-hens?

Molly brought a couple of her older chickens and some eggs, too, then spent hours bemoaning the fact that her hens had all taken to setting with this nice spring weather, so she'd have an abundance of chicks and no eggs. Wouldn't it be grand if hens could lay an egg every day?

Little baby Mary, nicknamed Molly, did not improve to Sam's satisfaction, but Susanna was delighted that the child could eventually sit unaided. She was such a bright thing, too; so winsome.

Came midsummer, and Susanna gave little Sammy a spell from his schooling. He was a perfectionist, even more so than she, and became frustrated and impatient at the least little flaw or error in his lessons. He needed a holiday. Susanna was amused to hear him speak with the cultured London accent, as she and Sam did. The lad seemed to be picking up none of the rural speech mannerisms in which he was immersed.

On her errands about town Susanna watched the village children at their games and antagonisms and fights. She didn't want that for her own little ones, but how could she prevent it? Young Sam would soon be old enough to be out and about the village, and perky, active Emilia would follow right on his heels.

She should think about hiring on another maid, too, debt or no. Little Molly needed frequent attention. Sammy should start lessons again soon, robbing part of her time from the others. And when this next baby arrived in a month or two, she would probably be slow, as usual, to recover.

She pondered all these nagging questions and forcibly refused to permit herself to wonder why God didn't make the way just a wee bit easier, as she walked upstreet this fine July day. Today she would put down a shilling on account at the baker's and buy four barley loaves. Molly perched more or less on the bulge. Sukey and Emilia clung to her skirts, for they still acted shy in the great wide world. No shy-boots, Sammy. He bounded ahead, greeted the dames at their gates, patted the dogs, and chattered like a jackdaw.

She had arrived at the baker's door when she saw Sam at the other end of the street, headed her way. She continued on to meet him; the baker could wait.

One of God's sweeter gifts is that of healing. Finally she could again greet her husband with a genuine smile. And yet, as with much of healing, a scar had remained, down in the darkness that could not be seen. The relationship between Sam and her had changed just the slightest bit. He almost certainly didn't notice it, but she felt it deep inside. Sam was no longer exactly perfect in her eyes. There was something of a tarnish, a patina, to his once brilliant halo. Or perhaps this was simply some effect that comes of growing older and wiser.

His active mouth was in the upturned position, something Susanna had not seen much of lately. "Do you remember the poem I wrote for William and Mary when they ascended?"

"All too well."

"I had ceased to think of it, but now I hear by post that before the queen died—rest her soul—she desired an appointment for the poet who had pleased her."

"Indeed! That was several years ago."

Sam's eyes danced. "Finally, apparently, an appointment has opened. Two hundred pounds a year, Sukey! Four times the income of this living!" He gripped her shoulders and squeezed. That was usually as close as he ever came to displaying affection in public; she considered it an accolade.

"Where?"

"Epworth!"

"That's not too far from here; still in Lincolnshire."

"On the strength of this letter I've already arranged a loan of a hundred and fifty pounds. With it we'll clear our debts and purchase a team and wagon. In fact, I know just the horses; I've had my eye on them for some while. We need a good team, and this is the perfect time to purchase." He was absolutely bouncing up and down, as if he had any sense about money at all.

"A hundred and fifty pounds' debt! To be paid off from a two hundred pound salary, as you raise this family."

"Fifty wasn't nearly enough, but this larger living? Handsome! Our money problems are over! Here." He gave her a pound note. "Clear us with the baker and butcher, and then choose something especially nice for dinner. We'll celebrate! A feast of thanksgiving, if you will."

"One pound won't do it."

He studied the note a moment as if disappointed by its puny lack of power. "Very well. Put it on account, and we'll pay the balance tomorrow."

"You have a hundred fifty pounds in hand right now?"

"No, of course not. No bank here in this hamlet. This is an advance against the full loan."

"An advance. As advanced by—?"

"The marquis." He said it as if it were something any marquis always did.

"Yes. The marquis." That deeply-buried scar tweaked. "The only man in town with any money. Is he perchance buying off the rector who preaches so loudly against vice?"

"I told you, the appointment came through the crown. Now go do your purchasing. I'll be home within two hours." Sam tousled little Sammy's hair and strode on down the lane.

Queen Mary had died, let's see—Susanna calculated—*two and a half years ago.* And Mary had mentioned a soft spot in her heart for the poet who charmed her back eight years ago. What an opportune time for Sam's new living to surface; at least, from the marquis's point of view.

Susanna brushed the thoughts to the back of her mind and turned toward the bakery. It didn't matter. Regardless of the circumstance, Sam's new appointment was most welcome. They would be in debt to bankers in the city, but that was better than being in debt to a dozen Mr. Stroods in this village. She could tuck away a bit each month unbeknownst to Sam and pay the debt off by degrees.

And it would have to be without Sam's knowledge, for every farthing that reached his hands slipped through his fingers like water. Smart Sam was a brilliant theologian, but when it came to managing money he was worse by far than her father.

And Sukey might be pretty, but she wasn't stupid.

9

Sadness at Epworth

Amid the thatched stone-and-clay cottages of Epworth stood occasional buildings of brick, some even with shake roofs. The population, Susanna had heard, was well in excess of two thousand—probably more like twenty-five hundred—with another thousand in the nearby farms and hamlets. Epworth had real shops, and its church of St. Andrew, Sam's new bailiwick, hardly looked its age at all. Epworth was no London, but neither was it wee South Ormsby.

Little Sammy put into motion his nonstop monologue of questions and comments. Emilia, the former babbler of the family, had no space left to insert her own constant commentary. That didn't slow her down, of course; toddlers thrive on cacophony. What would Susanna do when Sukey and Molly started talking? Make rules, that's what—strict rules regarding silence and conversation.

Was Epworth any more sophisticated than South Ormsby when it came to news and gossip? Probably not; it was still too small to be urbane. No doubt most of the curious eyes who noticed the Wesley wagon's passing knew that this was the new rector.

They passed St. Andrews and within the block arrived at the rectory. Silently, for the children were still devoted to filling the air with words, Susanna gave copious thanks to God. The rectory was three stories tall!

Sam sat with the lines loose in his hands and scanned the house with a critical eye. "Badly in need of repair."

"So large. At last; enough room."

"Going to have to replace some of the timbers in the barn. It's starting to lean."

"It's a barn. How far does our glebe extend?"

"I'm no farmer, but Hiram Wilkes back in South Ormsby could calculate the acreage of a piece of land shaped like a spilled pudding. I'd say, based on how Hiram did it, that we have a good two or three acres. Maybe a bit more, since the land dips away into that little glen."

Two or three acres of church land devoted specifically to the rector's use! "Sam, we can keep a couple cows, plant a garden—"

"You're no farmer either, Sukey."

"If I can master Greek and Hebrew I can learn to bury seeds and milk a cow. It will be an important saving for feeding the children."

"We don't have to worry so much about saving; two hundred pounds a year, remember?"

She skewered him with a sharp eye. "A hundred and fifty pound debt, remember? We will scratch and save until we're square with the world."

Was he angry? She watched his face.

No. His eyes twinkled. "Yes, mum!" Sam hopped to the ground. "Samuel, you'll help unload. So will you, Emilia. Ah. Here comes a welcoming committee, I trust. Sukey, you look white as bleached bones. Go sit. You've been overtaxed already."

Susanna didn't argue. She let Sam help her to the ground. Slowly, wearily, she settled herself beneath a gnarled old oak to rest. A delightful tree this, with sprawling branches and dark, hushed leaves. Susanna took a deep breath. Another. That was not the aroma of oaks or grass. She called to Emilia to mind the babies and climbed shakily to her feet to go exploring.

The rectory was half-timbered, its roof thatched. The clay between the timbers sloughed here and there; it really ought be patched before winter; but Susanna wasn't interested in the house itself just now. That aroma—

She paused by a creaky garden gate. The gate should be painted before winter, its latch mended. The latch was a project for little Sam. In fact, the painting just might be, too. She pushed through and out into the garden.

Yard-high tufts of grass obscured the paths. Weeds and ragged herbs fought for control of the herb beds. The dill was fallen over, the oregano scraggly, the rosemary completely died out. Someone had tried to raise roses without pruning them. Berry wands tangled with the unkempt rosebushes. That aroma— Susanna walked, not knowing exactly where and why, among the ruin to—to— Here it was, banked high along the back wall. Sweetbrier.

The courtyard and flower gardens of Spital Yard came rushing out from the past to smother her with memories. How often as a child had she marveled at its beauty. How often had her mother before her, in the midst of raising a sprawling family, taken a few quiet moments to bask in its sweetness.

Spital Yard. Sweetbrier. Epworth. Susanna had come full circle.

"Mother? The neighbors have brought a lovely stew, and a Mr. Cooper is starting a fire inside. Papa suggests you might come."

"Thank you, Sammy. I'm coming."

"Mother, are you crying?"

"No, dear, rejoicing." Susanna took her son's hand and started back toward the house, slowly, for the weariness was attacking fiercely. "The garden here should be put in order before autumn. That will be a first priority. How good are you at painting gates and mending latches?"

"Oh, may I?" His face brightened and sparkled, like his father's. He held the gate for her and pushed it more-or-less closed behind him.

"You'll pull your share of weeds, as well. Then when the bad weather descends upon us you'll go back to your schoolwork. You have made much

106

progress so far. This winter we'll tackle Latin and mathematics."

"I'm getting big, huh?"

"Very. Now here are the neighbors to greet us."

Before long Susanna was delivered of another girl, and she named her Mehetabel—Hetty. She liked the name partly because its translation was "God is doing good." Not only was God doing good in her life, to her the quintessence of God was to do good. And mostly, Susanna simply liked the way the name burst eagerly over the tongue and lips.

Then Susanna's world crumbled bit by bit. She had felt a certain frustration, an impatience, with the petty factions in South Ormsby. After all, the village wasn't that big. She was soon dismayed to learn that although Epworth was ten times the size of South Ormsby, its factions were a hundred times as strong. The local Whigs, known as isle men, sought to limit the power of the crown but couldn't even agree on what their party stood for. Sam, the enthusiastic Tory, faced stiff opposition in his congregation. All the nasty little side-taking and people-politics Susanna had endured in the past were multiplied in this cranky and miserable town.

The rectory, so in need of repair, remained in disrepair. Baby Hetty came before Susanna could put her little back garden in good order. She could see the sweetbriers out there beyond, but the herbs remained choked, the grass persisted.

Susanna wanted to rent out the glebe to good farmers, on shares. But Sam caught farming fever and eagerly went another fifty pounds into debt setting himself up as a farmer—and failing miserably as a farmer. A city man does not quickly succeed at an alien rural trade, for the skills of farming are as much inherited and absorbed as they are learned. The seed would not come to fruit simply because Sam the dreamer enthusiastically hoped it would.

The factions with which Susanna had to contend were far worse than she first surmised. The crown had decided to drain much of the swampy land nearby and make it suitable for farming. To do the task, the crown brought in Dutch engineers who knew a thing or two about drainage canals. The Dutchmen brought their own laborers, men paid handsomely, while the local men, poor to start with, lacked jobs and watched the project money fly away to the Netherlands.

To recompense the Dutchmen for their work, it was rumored, the crown determined to divide the new-made land into three portions; a third for the Dutchmen, a third for the crown, and a third for the local farmers. It was then that Epworth exploded.

Some begged to let things go whatever way they would. Others championed outright rebellion. Then all the minor factions lined up themselves between. No matter what Sam said from the pulpit, one group or another would misconstrue it. He could not win.

Nor could Susanna. She learned to her sorrow that most of the men in town could neither read nor write and almost none of the women were literate. That made both Sam and Susanna freaks from another world. Less than half grown, little Sammy was already better educated than any deacon in the church.

The locals might be illiterate, but they could count the shillings and pence—oh my, but they could! The two-hundred-pound debt shrank not a farthing. With time, it grew larger.

One expense was a maid. Illness plagued both the children and Susanna. She could not manage the household and five small children when she was bedridden.

Between the years 1697 and 1701, Susanna bore five more babies, including another set of twins.

All five died.

Her family had frozen in place, struggling but never growing. Sam's congregation listened to his preaching and failed to either repent or revive; the church kept struggling, never growing. Her little garden hung on, but she was usually too ill to tend it properly. It struggled with its weeds and neglect, hardly ever growing.

The normally ebullient Sam showed the strain. He studied his books and exercised his theology, preparing deep sermons to feed a hungry flock. The flock refused to eat. Almost to a man his congregation abhorred theology and despised book learning. If Sam couldn't even get his barley patch to come into head, he sure as sundown couldn't be trusted on issues that couldn't be seen.

Sam spent hours and days alone in his study writing rich and elaborate poetry. It didn't sell. In fact, the sort of poetry John Dunton had been so fond of calling doggerel didn't sell either.

Susanna watched Sam plan new sources of income, listened to him wax enthusiastic about some new project or idea. Their debt grew. In the hands of a prudent man, the living at Epworth would have supported the family adequately. Sam was not a prudent man.

One thing became increasingly clear. Life could not continue this way. Susanna saw no hope of changing Sam, nor could she see moving to some more urban parish in the near future—somewhere where Sam's profound insights and theological learning could be used and appreciated. Susanna could see that Sam was in the wrong place shepherding the wrong sort of people, but the church obviously didn't think so. Indeed, not even Sam noticed. He continued beating his head against stone walls, preaching repentance and book learning to people who could not even read.

Very well. If life as it was seemed difficult to endure, and neither Sam nor their circumstance would change, then Susanna must change. She would start with the farming.

The glebe had lain fallow for several years. Susanna purchased a couple of cows, shaggy little beasts with pretty horns and ragged brown coats, and turned them out onto her abandoned acreage to graze. She invited not one but two farm wives in for tea and from them learned the basics of cow care. From her own maid she learned how to milk them, should she be required to. She grew to like her cows immensely. Their big brown eyes were most appealing. But best of all they, like she herself, appreciated an orderly, methodical routine, with prompt milking at the same hour each day, week in, week out.

Now and then she would buy a shoat and raise it to butchering size. The pigs foraged across the glebe along with the cows and did especially well during acorn season. She dickered with the local farmers for vegetables from the fields, tops and husks still on, for a cheaper price than cleaned vegetables, then fed the pods and leavings to her pigs. She recalled how much she had hated dickering with the fishwives at Spital Yard. Oh, if she had only known!

She was reasonably successful raising chickens, much less so raising geese. A local huntsman sold her some shelducks he had captured in the fens, but she didn't know to clip their wing feathers again after moult, and they decided to live elsewhere.

The milk, meat, and eggs from her little farmstead helped out financially, but it still wasn't enough. She had been drifting away from God to an extent. Oh, true, she prayed each day and had taught the children the Lord's Prayer as soon as they could speak. But she didn't feel the old closeness, and she knew why. Very little personal study, very little meditation. And that condition she could change.

When she was very young (about age five?) she had vowed to God that for every hour she spent on pleasure she would spend an equal time on prayer and devotion. She had always kept that pledge, but these last few years, precious little time was left for pleasure. It was time to change the pledge.

She assigned two hours daily to meditation and devotion. It was very difficult at first, even with the help of her maid. Five small children do make demands, and she was teaching Sammy and Emilia six hours daily. But she had promised God two hours, and two hours He would get.

Her regimen of devotions did indeed bring her closer again to God, but it didn't help their living situation at all. Oh, how she yearned to live comfortably and free of debt! She had changed what she could and still that nagging dissatisfaction persisted. Might not God, prithee, work some changes also?

Change came, all right.

Susanna should have sensed it coming at morning prayers, as cold wind rattled the shutters and promised another dreary day. Sam went through his daily list of prayer subjects just as usual, but afterward she noticed him looking at her oddly, even suspiciously. He was definitely not his normal, cheerful self. If something was bothering him he would come out with it before too long; Sam could never hold a thing back.

It came out that very evening after family prayer. "Sukey, why didn't you say 'Amen' this morning to my prayer for our king?"

"You know my feelings. I believe the Prince of Orange to be a usurper. Mary had some claim, perhaps, but she's dead. A Stuart should be on the throne. Not William."

Sam's face tightened. Susanna tried to read subtleties in it as his thoughts moved but could not.

He glanced around at the children and stood up suddenly. "Come to my study."

"Bedtime, Sammy. Go tell the maid." Susanna shooed her firstborn off toward the kitchen and followed Sam to his study. She sat in the leather chair and folded her hands. She disliked political arguments; why could God not mate people with similar political views?

Sam wheeled on her. "William is king by divine right, and you dare say he shouldn't be."

"I believe in divine right as firmly as you. Romans thirteen: 'For there is no power but of God; the powers that be are ordained of God.'"

"And William is ordained by God."

"William was ordained by Parliament; hardly the same thing. God's will is expressed by bloodline, not Parliamentary notion, and William is not related by blood to the kingly line. There are Stuarts enough around to fill the throne."

His eyes crackled. "If that be the case, then we must part, for if we have two kings we must have two beds."

Susanna felt the heat rising in her neck. She was becoming angry at his blind stubbornness, and she couldn't stop herself. She tried to keep her voice flat, but it kept rising anyway. "I am well aware of your fondness for William. I read the elusive poetry you sent them when he and Mary first came to the throne. You've always been a William-enthusiast, if you will. But that doesn't make him worthy to be king; not with Mary dead. And I doubt very much that William cares whether you sleep in your wife's bed or not."

She regretted saying that last, but it was too late now.

Like ducks bursting up out of the marsh, Sam's ire exploded. His face flashed fire and triumph. He dropped to his knees, clasped his hands and stared ceilingward. "God in heaven," he intoned, "I pray Your judgment down upon my head if I should ever touch this woman or come into her bed before she has begged Your pardon and mine. Amen!"

Three lovely retorts came to Susanna's mind, but she kept them short of her tongue. Already she had done damage. She would maintain silence in the face of this buffoonery. That should serve as well as any rejoinder.

He climbed to his feet. "I believe that will be all. And now if you'll excuse me—" He sat at his desk and turned as much of his back to her as the angle of the desk permitted.

She stood. "If I'll excuse you indeed. There is no excuse for this overweening display."

His voice stopped her halfway to the door. "Feel free to knock and enter when you choose to beg pardon."

She glared at him. "My only error, for which I beg your pardon, was the use of 'overweening.' It's far too mild a term."

She refrained from slamming the study door behind her, but she closed it firmly. How dare he! And to try to force her lip service by threatening to withdraw his marital duties—? Right is right, and principles are principles. Susanna had never shirked her responsibility toward either right or principle. Nor would she now. She stomped upstairs.

She took her time preparing for bed. She still had most of her slim figure. Her face showed a few lines that hadn't been there before, but one must expect that at thirty-two years of age. No gray marred the rich raven color of her hair yet.

No, there was no reason to suspect Sam's interest might be flagging because his wife had turned flabby and frumpy. His inane vow to God tonight was pure bravado, a tongue temporarily out of control because of anger. His temper was like that. He had always been like that. Why should she expect moderation this time?

She crawled into her cold bed and lay very still until the covers warmed around her. The wind blew as hard as ever, beating its icy fists against the shutters.

Sam would be in eventually, once his anger cooled. She dozed fitfully. Weariness won, and she slept.

When she awoke at dawn Sam's side was still vacant. She dressed, arranged her hair with special care, and went downstairs. The household was just beginning to stir, following the patterns of activity it followed methodically every morning.

Sam's study door stood open. She stepped inside. He had left a sheet of foolscap on his otherwise cleared desk. It was a note in his hand, written a bit larger than usual. His duties as the convocation man for the diocese called, and he had no plans to return in the immediate future.

Sam had gone off to Lincoln.

10

The Finger of God

The crackly yellow envelope contained three one-pound notes. That was all. How far did Sam think three pounds was going to go when every merchant in town was dunning her for payment on accounts past due? She sighed and returned the notes to the comfort of their envelope. The March wind thrust its clammy fingers through the loose weave of her shawl. So far, March offered no promising smells or warm wafts as an earnest payment on the laggard spring. Indeed, the month was threatening to go out like a lion. She walked back into the house.

Sammy looked up from his slate beside the fire. "Is Papa returning soon?" He always asked that.

"No word yet." She always answered that. The boy had recently turned twelve. Susanna doubted he knew about the true nature of the marriage union—she certainly hadn't told him anything—but he was old enough to be aware of an unnatural separation when he saw it. It must bother him.

It surely bothered her.

Here came the maid, back early from shopping. She closed the door against the wind and whipped off her cape. "Gonna rain today yet; feels so. Big news, mum. King William died a week ago, on the eighth. Anne is queen." She paused; her voice assumed a cautious, hopeful note. "Isn't Anne a Stuart, mum? I mean, she's a proper queen, ain't she?"

"A proper queen, yes. And pray don't use 'ain't' before the children."

"Yes'm. Then there's no problem now, seeing you and master can agree upon who's queen, ain—isn't that so?"

"Let's devoutly hope so." Susanna set Emilia to work at her mathematics, drilled Molly in her letters and numbers, and listened to Sukey recite. All that busyness occupied the front of her mind. The back of her mind worried, as it had for the last five months.

Sam was being pigheaded and, in a way, Susanna was being just as pigheaded. And yet this was a matter on which she would not bend—she could not bend. William had been the thorn, and he was a thorn no longer. Or had he been? Was fealty to William at the root of this unfortunate schism, or did it go deeper, perhaps past mending?

Easter would fall on April 5 this year. Easter was the season of renewal, the celebration of life both eternal and temporal. Surely things would be healed by then. This argument, started so simply, had continued far too long already, like a fire out of control. No, like an icy storm out of control, freezing both soul and spirit.

As Susanna had feared, March was slow and surly about letting go of winter. Easter Sunday was still raw. A rather uncaring young curate, his theology as sloppy as his dress, celebrated the Easter services, for Sam had gone to London.

A few days later, bitterly frustrated, Susanna wrote a letter to Dr. George Hickes. Persecuted for years for both his religious and his political beliefs, the man had earned her respect, and she knew Sam respected him as well. Perhaps a wisdom greater than hers and Sam's could prevail.

She mentioned the name of the woman who had recommended him, her friend Lady Yarborough. She laid out her own argument and, as best she could, Sam's. She appealed to him to intervene if possible, to advise if intervention were unwise. And then she waited for the post and remembered the days when she memorized the hoofbeats of the post horse as she awaited letters from her true love Samuel.

Young love. That headstrong young love had aged and mellowed. Her love was different now. Was it there at all? She had to search her heart, but yes, it was. For all his iron-headedness and lack of money acumen, she loved him. They argued every point of view, didn't even see eye-to-eye on child-rearing, and yet she loved him. She yearned for his companionship; she needed his cheeriness when life got very heavy. And she yearned for his arms again. It had been too, too long.

On the twenty-ninth of the month Dr. Hickes's reply reached her. Her hopes and spirit, so chilled by the whole affair, warmed perceptibly. Dr. Hickes was on her side!

"Samuel's oath," he wrote, "is inconsistent with his marriage vows and is therefore invalid. It was perjury for him to make the vow, and will be a continuance of perjury for him to persist in the performance of it. I advise you consult the Archbishop of York and Bishop of Lincoln and request them, if they agree with me that the oath is unlawful, to charge him to loose himself from the bond of sin, by which he cannot bind himself by the law of God and man. I encourage you, even if this fails, to stand firm."

Stand firm. Susanna was a specialist in standing firm, although lately she had found it more and more difficult. This advice of Dr. Hickes buoyed her up and gave her starch not even daily devotions could provide.

Stand firm. Easy for the doctor to say. So difficult to do. In a terse note accompanied by too little money, Sam refused to accept the arbitration of any outside opinion. And he mentioned seeking a chaplaincy aboard a man-of-war. Susanna tried to see the advantage of such a thing. Sam would be making a nice wage, and it would be sent directly to her, Sam being at sea. With only herself to manage the funds, and Sam an ocean away from anyplace to spend it, she might even get their finances into some semblance of order.

120

Sam an ocean away. She spent the afternoon dissolved in tears and at evening devotions felt no better for having cried the day away than she felt before.

She had acknowledged that the whole morass could be mended only by God Himself, but she had never really let go. For the first time in her life, Susanna Annesley Wesley gave up. Sam was adamant; so was she. Her position was correct according to the laws of God. Dr. Hickes agreed with that. The crux was no longer who sat on the throne of England. Sam's vow had become the problem. She saw that clearly enough, and he could persist in it only with God's tacit approval. Susanna would sit back and let God work His own way.

On May fifteenth she wrote a letter to that effect to Lady Yarborough.

In the midst of the mess she gave birth to a daughter, her fourteenth child. Queen Anne was a legitimate ruler; Queen Anne's accession should have solved this tragic dilemma, had stubbornness not frozen it past solution. Susanna named her baby Anne.

July. The sun came early and stayed late. Summer warmth helped soften memories of the harsh and bitter spring. Susanna suspended the children's lessons for a spell. And her sweetbrier came into flower at long last.

She was unusually slow to bounce back from this birthing. After weeks abed, she was finally garnering enough energy to take quiet walks around the garden.

This particular evening she wandered out through the freshly painted gate into her somewhat orderly garden. The weeds had been beaten back along the paths here, but the grass and thistles and pigweed in the rear had yet to be pulled. She'd get Molly onto that job. Molly's crippling deformities made her a natural for sitting-down jobs. The child was six now and ready for chores.

Here was her sweetbrier, coming into its glory. She inhaled deeply. Ahhh. When life became burdensome, a little fragrance meant a lot. She thought of how God must find human foibles burdensome, and how He must relish the fragrance of His obedient servants. "We are unto God a sweet savor of Christ." Where was that? Second Corinthians, she thought.

A footstep on the path behind her made her turn. She caught her breath. "Sam."

"Sukey." His riding clothes were all dusty. He must have just arrived.

She ached to embrace him. She held her place, rigid. "You've seen our newest?"

"Anne, Emilia tells me. She's a lovely baby."

"One of our prettiest." She licked her lips. She must tread carefully here, most carefully. "I assumed Anne was a name we would both agree upon."

"Yes, as, I assume, we both agree on the legitimacy of the queen." He wandered off to study the lily plants. "Your lilies aren't blooming."

"Too early. Next month."

He continued on, pausing by the rosemary bush in the shelter of the west wall. "Where rosemary flourishes the mistress rules."

Susanna had heard that adage many a time. Nor was it the only one she knew. "Who passes by the rosemary and cares not to take a spray, for women's love no care has he nor shall he, though he live for aye."

Sam twisted to study her a moment. His eyes danced; the creases in their corners deepened. What was he thinking? He plucked a sprig of rosemary, held it to his nose and inhaled deeply, then tossed the spray to her. He continued his circuit of the garden.

She caught the sprig with two hands. Its leaves had been bruised by the plucking. Its aroma overwhelmed her memory of the sweetbrier's. She was a practical woman, a direct woman, and not one to dance so daintily among the roses. "Let us stop skating around the edges of the pond and go straight to the middle. Are you here to stay?"

"That depends." He wheeled to face her. "Are you ready to submit your will to mine in every regard, as a proper wife must?"

"What you're saying is, am I willing to abandon any opinions of my own? There was a day when you valued my opinions, whether they reflected yours or not. Have I ceased being a person at some time between that day and this?"

"The husband is head and master of the house. You refuse to accept that."

"You have always been head and master. In fact, I daresay if you were not in charge of finances we wouldn't be over two hundred and fifty pounds in debt right now. I may not agree with your choice of king or your notions of discipline, but they prevail nonetheless. Yours are the prayers the children hear—when you're around to offer them."

"You're begging the issue. I'm talking about the true submission a wife must make."

"No. No, there's more. I can't believe this tiff is the whole reason for your actions. We spent over twelve years in marriage together; surely this isn't the first you noticed that our opinions vary. Are you looking for an excuse to get away? Are Lincoln and London that much nicer to be in than Epworth?"

His face, already tight, twisted more. It spoke more than words could ever say. He turned away from her, back to the barely budding lilies. "They respect me there. I'm convocation man; I run the show. When I discuss the symbolism in Job they listen. I can sit in a coffeehouse and talk about a book I've read, and someone else has read it, too. No one here even knows how to read, let alone discuss anything beyond the weather and the price of eggs and barleycorn."

"I remind you you weren't given this parish by men. It was ordained of God. You belong here."

He walked slowly up the path to inspect the lavender. Its brittle aroma conquered the meager odor of the rue beside it. "For years I have preached revival. Renewal. There is no revival here in this God-forsaken wilderness. Just ignorance. Ignorant men who prize their ignorance and loathe anything better for themselves. They pay lip service to God and oppose me. If I belonged here I would have received some sign by now."

"You said you had applied for a ship's chaplaincy. Do you suppose that's where you belong?"

"Perhaps. I've not withdrawn my application." He turned to look at her finally. "You'd be well cared for. My salary would go to you, and you've been holding it up to me that you could manage better. This can be your chance to prove it."

"Unless you're lost at sea. Then I'm destitute, with six small children, no roof, and a burden of debt. Is that what you want for your son and daughters?"

"I want revival, Sukey. And it won't come here at Epworth."

"So you'll launch a revival at sea, one ship at a time." She was beginning to feel giddy again. She walked past him to the bench beside the sweet woodruff and sat down. "I've been writing letters, as you know—Lady Yarborough and George Hickes. Dr. Hickes urged me to take my appeal to the archbishop and bishop. I haven't yet. I would ask that we submit our problem to referees, one of whom—"

"No! I refuse to submit anything to outside persons. This is between you and me. Us alone. Not outsiders."

"Not your own masters the bishop and archbishop?"

"No reference of any sort."

"Very well. Then I suppose there's nothing more to talk about. I do ask that you read Dr. Hickes's reply to my letter. You should know what others think in the matter whether you consent to arbitration or not. And perhaps before dinner you might spend some time with Sammy. He asks about you."

He stood very close to her; his shadow fell across her face. "You make this whole problem out to be my fault somehow—that I'm the one being unreasonable. Had I my Bible in my hand I'd wag it in your face. The finger of God points to you, Sukey! To *you!*" He marched off to the house.

The finger of God. Yes. She would make the finger of God the topic of her devotions this evening.

Was she the problem? *Was* she really the one? Despite some doubts, the more she examined that possibility, the less she believed it. He was trying to escape a less-than-ideal rectorship in a dull and dreary parish. It was he, not herself.

She saw this, also: she could never sway him, and he would listen to no other voice. She must leave the matter to God. God took care of ravens and lilies of the field. He'd take care of her children; she must trust Him. Have faith. God would resolve this matter to His satisfaction. She must trust Him to.

Sam stayed two days—"putting things in order," he said. He stayed upstairs in Sammy's room. He had vowed not to touch her again until she begged God's pardon and his, and he was sticking to his vow. She certainly had to give his stubbornness its due.

Early the next morning, as the cock robins announced dawn and the jackdaws were picking through the pig's scraps, Sam left for London. Permanently.

Susanna cried through most of her morning devotional. Having him near but not with her hurt worse than when he was fifty miles away in Lincoln or two hundred miles away in London. To almost smell his closeness, to watch his hands move, to hear his voice—it tantalized. It stirred her. Didn't he feel anything? Was everything gone between them? Apparently.

At least she wasn't pregnant again. Mrs. Whipple up the street claimed that Susanna's ill health came of being pregnant constantly. The woman was illiterate and unschooled in spiritual matters, but she knew more than doctors about keeping well. If she was right, Susanna at least would enjoy better health when she was turned out on the street.

She completed her devotions, with difficulty, an hour later than usual; she would not let wandering thoughts rob her of godly thinking. She sent Molly and Sukey out to weed the herb patches by the east fence, then had to go out and show them what to pull and what to save. She sent Sammy to dig the thistles, for the girls refused to touch them.

She sent the maid downstreet for more bread; with Sam home those few days the usual ration of bread had gone too quickly. Having sent people off in all directions, she herself walked out to the barn to check on the dark cow's infected udder. Then she took up her sewing and strolled out to the bench by the sweet woodruff to mend the tear in Sammy's other britches.

Globby clouds scudded off-and-on across the sun, keeping the day cool. The rent was worse than she had thought. She pricked herself with the needle. Twice. This day was going morbidly, as might be expected when your man has left for good. She was near tears again. She really should not cry in front of the children.

Across her fell a shadow darker than that which the clouds made. Sam had returned! She laid her work in her lap and watched his face.

The children saw him, of course, and came running. He said fatherly things, hugged them, and sent them back to their labors.

"Sukey, do you remember the old clergyman who sometimes rides down through this way?"

"I do."

"As I was riding out the road this morning he was riding in. We spoke a few minutes, and the topic fell on my leaving, and the reasons for it. In short, he prevailed upon me to return and fulfill my responsibilities as pastor. He claims the curates the church sends out here aren't suitable."

"He's right. Shallow young men, slipshod theology. Mouth opinions about local politics of which they know nothing. They've turned the locals further against you just by being associated with St. Andrews."

"As he says also." Sam nodded, hesitated. "And so I've returned as rector. Only."

"Your vow. Dr. Hickes says, and I agree, that your vow is invalid because it's contrary to the vow you made at our wedding."

"I won't back down." His voice almost broke. "I can't."

"I rather wish, if that be the case, that you weren't here."

Susanna went to bed early that night but her weary body refused to fall asleep.

She heard the stairs creaking. Sam was coming up at last. The squeaky board in the hall floor beyond their chamber told her he had walked on. The stairs to the third floor groaned quietly. He would be in Sammy's room tonight.

She slept then, after another spell of weeping. She awakened to children's voices in the distance crying, "Fire!" What did children know about fire? A child was shaking her and tugging at the blanket. A whoosh of cold air rushed in with every tug. She gathered the blanket closer around.

"Mama, fire! Get up!" The squeaky voice finally penetrated. Emilia pulled the blanket away and yanked her arm.

"What—?"

Sam's strong arms dragged her bodily across the floor; they pressed her against his warm, broad chest. She snatched at the blanket and wrapped it around herself.

He paused by the chamber window and shouted at the night blackness in the front yard. "Sam! Is Molly out?"

"Yes, Papa!"

Susanna stumbled, half walking, half being carried, across the room to the door.

The hallway was full of smoke. They made their way down the stairs more by memory than by feel. Behind them something came crashing in.

Her lungs and eyes burned; heat blasted her face. She could hear nothing but roar and crackling, could see nothing at all. An orange hell filled her pleasant kitchen. Flames blocked the garden door. They pushed past the butter churn to the rarely-used stairwell door. It was warped shut. Sam turned her loose long enough to slam a bulky shoulder into it. It popped open.

Susanna ran forward, and then Sam's arms were around her again, pulling her along faster than she could go. Cold, dark night air swamped her and sapped away the heat. They ran.

"Gather around!" The voice of the master of the house boomed solidly, reassuringly.

Here in the dull orange glow stood the wild-eyed maid with baby Anne in her arms. Sammy with Molly; tiny Hetty clinging to Emilia; Sukey—

All accounted for.

Neighbors were shouting and running, coming from all directions. Susanna knew better than to think this an outpouring of community sympathy; they feared the fire would reach their own houses were it not stopped.

She found herself crying in the midst of her harsh coughing. She tried to stop; she couldn't. Sam's warm, broad hand pressed her wet face against him as he cooed platitudes of some sort.

Thunder brought her head snapping around; part of the roof had just caved in. A hideous blast of sparks and tiny yellow flames shot up into the blackness and winked out one by one as they drifted down. Windows glowed orange; shutters flew outward as fire like the breath of dragons blew them open.

She pushed away from him. Platitudes! Is that what he offered? "This!" She sobbed and jabbed her hand toward her ruined home. "This, Sam Wesley, is what the divine Judge thinks of your vow. *This* is the finger of God!"

11

The Isle Men

"**S**am?" Susanna snuggled closer and listened for signs of restlessness in the black night beyond their bed. Three children slept in this room with Sam and Susanna. All quiet. All asleep.

A gentle arm slipped across her shoulders. "Mmm?"

"I think perhaps I'm pregnant again."

"Boy this time?"

"I'll see what I can do."

The arm gave an affectionate squeeze. "I look forward to the house getting finished and children sleeping in their own rooms again. Did you talk to the carpenters today?"

"They tell me repairs will be complete by Christmas."

"They said the house would be done by All Hallows, too."

"I believe them this time. They're as anxious to finish as we are. The isle men are giving them grief for working for us. Sam? Do you suppose those ruffians set the fire?"

"Quite possibly." He was looking at her through the blackness. "I thought it was the finger of God."

"Someone mortal had to throw the faggot. Don't tease me. We promised mutually not to mention that episode, remember?"

He drew in close again. "Think we'll ever be able to get rid of the burnt smell?"

"I doubt it. I almost wish the place had burned to the ground, except for our books and papers. Then at least we'd start with the smell of fresh wood instead of stale smoke and char."

"I've learned from this," Sam said. "I think now I can accept better where I'm put; no matter where that might be. God placed me here, so here I am. I had trouble with that simple bit; always wanted to be elsewhere. I believe maybe now I can even put up with your constant, infernal sense of order and routine."

Christmastide passed, and the house finally stood more or less completed. New-hewn timbers and fresh clay plaster hardly masked the odor of fire that pervaded and remained. Eleven months after the fire, when the baby arrived, that odor still came sneaking out from odd corners of the house now and then to remind her of the horror of that night.

The baby was a boy, and he quickly received a pet name, as had each of the other children. Mary was Molly around the house and Samuel Junior just plain Sammy. Little Susanna was Sukey as Susanna herself had been, and Hetty flowed naturally from Mehetabel. Anne had become Nancy. This one would be John Benjamin Wesley, Susanna's only child with a middle name, the John and the Benjamin names of babies that had not survived. The world at large could address her new boy properly as John, but to her he was Jackie.

Early the following spring, as Jackie was just beginning to crawl, Sam planted flax over much of the glebe. With uncharacteristic interest in farming, Sam quizzed the neighbors about flax growing. For the first time in years Susanna saw in him a renewal of interest in the rectory itself and its lands. Good. If this flax crop brought them closer to freedom from debt, perhaps Sam would feel less restless, less inclined to go roaming in Lincoln and London.

The summer deteriorated as petty politics again tore the isolated community apart. Susanna was beginning to become impatient with the nonsense. Were they arguing politics on a national level, or considering problems of pan-European import, she might see their zeal. Pettiness, however, irritated her. It was disorderly for no reason. Irrationality, though, did not make the local situation any less dangerous.

With his usual enthusiasm Sam had hired a tutor for Sammy, and with equal enthusiasm he booted the fellow out when the man's predilection for wine and spirits surfaced. The boy was fourteen now. Susanna had schooled him well in all she knew, and Sam had taught him languages. He was ready to go on, one way or another. The tutoring had fallen through; the other way was school in Westminster.

Susanna committed the boy to God's care, in whose care he had been all along anyway, made him an extra shirt, and sent him off. Her firstborn was still fresh from the cradle, nowise big enough to go off on his own to London. The thought depressed her for weeks.

With the heat of August, tempers quickened and the flax ripened, pretty much simultaneously. "The fibers are at their best," Sam announced, "when the seeds are just starting to swell. We must watch for the first pods to begin turning yellow."

Hetty and Molly, seven and eight now, took it upon themselves to check the flax. Susanna received daily reports. Sam received daily reports, too, on the grumbles and threats of his enemies, the isle men. "And why not? We ourselves are an island of Tories in a restless ocean of Whigs," he would muse, and shrug it off. Susanna was not so certain the situation was shruggable.

Should Sam scythe his flax down or pull it? Pull it, said the neighbors; more fiber of better quality. When should he pull it? On the morrow, said the neighbors.

That night as Susanna was passing Emilia's open door she saw a soft yellow glow from the window beyond. She ran to the window. "Sam!" she shrieked. "The glebe!"

From his study downstairs Sam heard. From abed the children heard, for little feet came running together with the big ones.

Susanna jogged downstairs, ran out the garden door, and raced down the carriage lane past the barn.

In the darkness at the far end of the field, down in the corner by the glen, bright orange flame boiled up through clouds of smoke tinted glowing yellow. Here came neighbors from all sides with brooms and blankets. A dozen men and women began beating at the edges of the blaze, anxious that it might spread to their own flax and hay.

A stiff breeze was dragging the fire this way, straight across the flax field. Susanna snatched Emilia's counterpane off the clothesline and ran out across the field barefoot. The barn, with her cows and pig and chickens—it mustn't reach the barn!

The flax was nearly four feet tall out here—almost armpit high on Susanna. Weeds and flax stems bound her ankles and caught in her toes, slowing her to a ragged walk. Acrid smoke rolled ahead of the flames. Suddenly she could neither breathe nor see. Blindly, wildly, she flailed with the counterpane at the crackling noise in front of her. She tried to back up and tangled in the unwieldy snarl of stalks. She turned and fled from the smoke.

Men with shoes were trampling a fireline down beyond the blaze. Susanna fell back to the line and began ripping flax stalks away from the fireline, widening it, putting loose dirt between flame and fuel. Over there the fire jumped the line. With much shouting two men stomped a new line.

137

It was getting darker. Susanna realized gradually that the fire was smaller. Black gaps in the angry yellow wall yawned wider and wider. Here came Clyde Willis with his yoke of oxen dragging a log or beam of some sort. He drove them out along the jagged line where flame ended and green began. Little puddles of light here and there snuffed out beneath his drag.

And then, almost as an afterthought, the world grew quiet; no shouts and cries, no crackling flame, no thrashing and crashing. One of the oxen lowed a request to go home. Silent people stood about in the darkness. It seemed hard to understand, after the wild and frantic fight, that it was over.

They had won, but only barely. Susanna stood less than twenty feet from her barn.

When Susanna woke next morning before dawn, Sam was already gone from bed. She didn't bother with her hair. She pulled on an old dress and hurried downstairs. Her feet hurt, and no wonder. A dozen cuts and scuffs on them reminded her she had gone running through the field barefoot. She was barefoot now.

She left the house through the garden door. The sky was in its usual state—overcast and murky. She paused by the barn, searching. There stood Sam in the midst of the destruction, his whole body drooping in a dejected slouch. Most of his field had burned flat and black. Stinking curls of smoke still lifted off the smoldering ruin here and there. The plants that had not burned lay trampled and bruised.

Sam watched her come wading through crushed flax. She stumbled in beside him, and he put a brawny arm around her.

"So," he purred, "we're no worse off than we were when the field lay fallow."

"And no better. This was going to ease our debt. It could have helped us greatly." Her eyes burned—and not from smoke. "The fire in the house might have been an accident, but this can't possibly be. You know the magistrates won't look very deeply into the matter; they're the staunchest of Whigs."

" 'Vengeance is mine,' says the Lord. 'I shall repay.' Don't you think about helping Him."

She snorted. "I wouldn't mind being His willing tool."

North wind and harvest together with autumn rain dampened the heat of political acrimony. Susanna looked forward to a quiet winter.

It stayed quiet only until the approach of elections in 1705. Then the isle men and the moderates and the few Tories, Sam among them, had at it anew. As the grass sprouted green, angry voices took up again the arguments muted by the winter. Factions divided so severely that people stood in political clusters around the maypole on May Day.

The second week of May Susanna gave birth to her sixteenth baby. Maybe Mrs. Whipple the health sage was right; twenty-three months separated Jackie's birth and this child's, and both the infant and Susanna came through the ordeal well. Susanna would employ an extra nurse for the first few months, for although she was not prostrated she was very weak, but she felt better this time than she had with some. Perhaps the Lord wouldn't take this baby away so soon.

Elections were scheduled for the thirtieth of the month, and they couldn't come a moment too soon for Susanna. She was heartily sick of all the fuss. Some of the more voluble isle men even shouted threats at her children playing in the rectory yard.

Tuesday evening the twenty-ninth Sam left for a meeting in Lincoln. Susanna hated to see him go. Still, election day was an extremely sensitive time for a Tory to go walking in this dark Whig forest. With Sam the irritant gone, perhaps the isle men and their ilk would forget about pestering the rectory.

They didn't. Most of election eve, clear into the wee hours, they gathered outside the rectory close to the bedroom window and made noise. Hideous noise, constant noise—they fired muskets, beat on tin pans and drums, and described loudly and graphically their opinion of people who support a heartless monarch.

Susanna sent the maid out to tell them Sam wasn't home, but either they didn't believe her or Susanna, too, was an object of hatred and ridicule.

With every gunshot the baby jerked. Three-year-old Nancy crept, sobbing, into bed with Susanna. In consternation Susanna sent Nancy to Emilia's bed and asked the new nurse to take the baby to her house for the balance of the night. The poor little thing was a nervous wreck at only three weeks of age. Then Susanna buried herself in goose down and counterpanes and tried to rest.

When did the rascals finally quit? Susanna didn't know. The only noise-makers outside her window now were the robins, hedge sparrows, and linnets tuning up for their dawn concert. She heard a muffled cry from somewhere downstairs. No matter; let the regular maid handle it. Susanna drifted away again, floating warm and free in that comfortable world between deep sleep and the full awakening of morning.

Someone stood near her bed snuffling. Susanna tried to force herself closer to wakefulness. Her body chided her and refused to arouse itself.

"Mum—?" the maid's voice cracked.

"Mmph. What?"

"The babe, mum—"

"Can't you handle it?"

"Please, mum." The maid sobbed.

Susanna arched around stiffly and pulled her body up. The maid plopped a dead weight in her lap and literally ran from the room.

What did they have wrapped in the baby's blanket that they would—?

Susanna screamed even though her mind refused to take in what she saw. Her whole being was disjointed, each member acting independently, none of her faculties really admitting that the bundle in her lap was what it was—her baby. Dead.

She screeched out the maid's name.

The terrified woman hovered in the doorway. "Mum—?" She sobbed again, and her face was wet. "The woman—the nursemaid, mum. Them political freaks last night was so loud so long, mum, that she got over-tired. 'Tis their fault, mum, and none of hers, that she slept too hard. She laid on the baby she says, mum, had it in her bed with her as y'd do with a newborn, and she laid on it and snuffed it. Oh, mum! Hit wasn't meant."

Susanna heard herself send the woman away. She wrapped her arms around her newborn and cradled it, rocked it, hugged it. By slow and painful degrees her head, and then her heart, accepted what had happened.

By evening she had gathered her wits sufficiently to arrange the infant's burial.

They probably had fired her house. They most definitely had torched Sam's flax. And now—the maid was right—they were responsible for her baby's death. Ghastly wretches, repugnant in God's eyes and hers. Politics! How she hated politics. To cause such heavy sorrow and loss—

What more could those isle men do to her beleaguered family?

A few weeks later they got Sam arrested and sent to debtors' prison.

12

A Brand from the Fire

Susanna clasped and unclasped her hands nervously. It wasn't the surroundings that made her nervous. She didn't mind massive city structures, for she'd been born and raised in London, and York, though smaller, was nearly as urbane. She didn't mind coming face-to-face with an archbishop; her own father had been a man of eminence in contact with important personages. She grew up surrounded by great men and great thinkers.

What made her nervous was the topic of this audience. Sam had first approached the Archbishop of York five years before and for the same reason—to beg money. Sam had received twenty pounds from the man and, with a London trip and a few other unaffordable extravagances, the money had evaporated even before Susanna had seen it. Now here she was on the prelate's doorstep.

The archbishop's aide entered the far end of the long hall. "Milady, His Grace will see you now."

Susanna followed the young man out through ornately carved mile-high doors. She expected the archbishop to be seated on some sort of throne-like chair on an elevated dais from which he could peer down upon an humble rector's wife. But no. They walked out into a pleasant little walled garden.

Forget-me-nots lined the well-groomed paths with their soft, gentle blue. Primroses splashed their gay colors against the feet of the cabbage roses along the east wall. And here, mounded up against the rockwall, sprawled the dark-green tangle of sweetbrier. Susanna paused as inconspicuously as possible to fill her nose and heart with the rich, clinging aroma of its first flowering. The familiar old-home scent bolstered her courage and restored the confidence she had enjoyed as a youngster, when she knew all the answers. Oh, true, God was with her; but surely God was with the Archbishop of York as well.

His title sounded imposing, lofty, and yet the man himself was nothing like that. He sat on a wooden chair near a sundial, with neatly trimmed privet at his back, and he smiled at her approach.

She performed the appropriate obeisance for an archbishop and instantly worried that it hadn't been appropriate enough. It was done now. It would have to do.

"Do be seated, Mrs. Wesley. Let's not dwell on formality." He motioned toward a stool before him. She thanked him and perched on the stool, no less nervous because he seemed so approachable, and clasped her hands firmly to make them behave.

"I heard," he began, "that our Samuel is in debtor's prison in Lincoln. I heard also that you sent him your rings, the only thing of value you own, for fear he wasn't getting enough to eat."

She felt her cheeks get warm. "He returned them; said that wasn't necessary. Perhaps I overreacted."

The august gentleman leaned back and laced his fingers together, much as Papa had once done. Susanna got the vague feeling that she ought to be sitting at this man's feet. "Tell me please, Mrs. Wesley; have you ever really wanted for bread?"

"Strictly speaking, my lord, no. Not want. But then, it's so much trouble to get food before it's eaten and then to pay for it after, that it's misery for me. I think to have food on those terms is the next degree of wretchedness to having none at all."

He was looking at her with large, soft eyes, the way Papa once did. "You have five children at home here?"

"Samuel Junior is away at school in London. A bright boy; he's fifteen now. There are six others at home yet, ages two to thirteen. We would have a newborn now, except—" Words failed her. When words came, they were the wrong ones. "—except that we're Tories."

She bit her lip. She hadn't meant to mention the matter at all. But that pain her body felt for its lost baby was still too fresh, the wound in her spirit still too new. It all tumbled out; the fires, the harassment, the constant opposition—and lastly, the cows and dog.

"Shortly after Sam was arrested—in his churchyard, I might add—vandals damaged the church. There was talk of locking it, but the magistrates decided better of it. And the cows. Not long after Sam was taken away, someone slashed our cows during the night. Slashed their milk bags, cut their udders. The dog must have tried to defend them. He was stabbed, too, a leg nearly cut off. The cows are alive; it takes more than that to kill a cow, I understand; but they're useless for milking. We need the milk, Your Grace."

He sat quietly for long moments, and Susanna was glad. She could use the time to compose herself. He drew in a bucketful of air. "What would you have me do, Mrs. Wesley?"

"I don't know. I don't know what you might do, nor what I can do, for that matter. Sam is determined to stay; he's accepted that God has put him there in Epworth. But what next?" She shook her head.

He smiled. "I've been getting mail."

She frowned a moment until the light dawned. "Of course. Letters of complaint from Sam's enemies."

"In part, yes. He preaches renewal and revival, I take it. The letters don't agree with each other, but between the lines I detect that your Samuel is pricking consciences. As well he should; it's his job. And they complain of his politics."

"I am assuming your politics and Sam's coincide."

"Quite. Also I received a letter from Samuel himself. From the prison." He dug into the tightness of his cincture and pulled out a folded sheet of foolscap. "Let's see. He mentions his enemies burning his flax; quite disappointed to lose his flax it seems. He's dabbling in farming?"

"Dabbling. Yes. The flax was his pride, and it was indeed coming well. The field had lain fallow, in pasturage for several years, and was fertile."

He nodded, smiling. "Quote: 'One of my biggest concerns was my being forced to leave my poor lambs in the midst of so many wolves.' And later: 'My wife bears it with that courage which becomes her, and which I expected from her.' Then he goes on to talk about his ministry inside the prison walls. He's pleased God is using him among the men who need God so desperately. Talks about the good he can do there." The archbishop folded the paper. "And that delights me more than you know—to have a man in my bishopric so totally devoted to God."

What could she say? "His constant prayer is for revival. He's certain it will come, somehow."

The prelate stood, smiling. "Mrs. Wesley, I enjoyed this visit. You say you don't know what to do, and yet you're doing it. I receive reports of your exceptionally well-mannered children. Rearing children in the fear of the Lord is an awesome responsibility, as is maintaining this rectory in your husband's frequent absences. And now, I believe

I've thought of a few things I might do." He produced an envelope and pressed it into her hand. "This is one of them. A church fund established just for such occasions. I shall be in touch."

The aide escorted her out, past the sweetbrier. She walked in a sort of haze, that envelope in her hand. It was some minutes before she had collected her wits enough to open it.

The envelope contained a gift, a generous gift. It wasn't enough to buy Sam's freedom, but it would hold the wolves at bay and bring bread to the table for the next few weeks. Bread and milk. Who could be so vindictive as to slash her cows and the family's dog?

She thought back on the conversation, trying to trace its nuances through her memory. She could tell one thing: from the gentleman's tone of voice and his avuncular mien, he was on Sam's side in this unholy war of nerves and cowardly sorties. The man's firmness of voice suggested to her also that when he spoke of "some things to do" on Sam's behalf he would do them.

Some weeks later the archbishop managed by subscription to pay off about half Sam's debt load. Sam was home by Christmas, then away for the balance of the winter as proctor to the London convocation.

Susanna found herself writing frequently and long to Sammy, and Sammy through his responses seemed to welcome her letters. "I would advise you to arrange your affairs by a certain method," she wrote, "by which means you will learn to improve every precious moment."

Come summer of 1706 Susanna surprised herself, if not the world, by not giving birth. Early 1707, however, brought Martha, who became Patty around the house.

A week before Christmas in 1707, months before her due date, Susanna gave birth untimely to a boy. He was such a fragile thing, and tiny. She had lost all her other premature boys. She made the desirability of sons a major theme of devotion and prayer. Perhaps God would be gracious and spare this child. She named him Charles.

Charles lived and grew, although he was excessively slow to gain weight. But once he outgrew the setback of an early birth he became by many measures her brightest, cheeriest, and prettiest child—and most active! By February of 1709 he was walking at a dead run and getting into everything.

Wednesday, February 9, seemed like any other Wednesday during the final throes of a pregnancy. Susanna spent the day in bed, too sick to care if the world continued or not. She could by now fully appreciate the constant illness her own mother had endured. Her mother had borne twenty-five. This was Susanna's nineteenth. Were the men to bear the children, every family would have but one.

John wasn't quite six yet, Patty but two, and there went Charles at full gallop. The maid was getting run ragged and Emilia at seventeen couldn't carry the full load. Perhaps they should hire a second girl. And yet their finances would hardly allow it. Their debt still weighed too heavily.

Politics heated up again. Susanna could do without that. At least Sam was home for the moment.

Dinner came as usual at six, but Susanna couldn't eat anything. She sipped at a glass of wine and didn't even finish that. Despite the Bible's suggesting a little wine for Timothy's stomach's sake, she had sharply curtailed her usual intake of drink. Perhaps this was one of God's checks and balances; that if she were healthier she would drink too much.

The house dropped silent at eight. Somewhat later Sam came padding up from his study, kissed her good night, and retired to the room next door. Why couldn't she sleep well? Her mind and body refused to settle into ease. She felt vaguely dissatisfied, restless. She wasn't going to go into labor prematurely again, was she? No, Lord, please—not another early, difficult birth.

In the blackness beyond the door, Hetty's soprano voice screeched. The door burst open. "Mama, fire! Pieces of fire fell by my feet!"

"Your father—"

Hetty was gone. Susanna heard the girl pound on Sam's door, heard Sam's voice and heavy footfalls.

Here were Emilia and Sukey in the darkness, but it wasn't dark anymore. An orange glow, that hideous orange glow of a prior nightmare, lighted the doorway. As Susanna and her girls staggered out into the hall Sam broke in the nursery door shouting.

The wall beside her, already hot, burst into a solid sheet of flame. Susanna shrieked. Somehow one foot flung itself ahead the other and propelled her down the stairs. Emilia was gone; now she was back with a steadying hand.

Here was Sam; they'd be fine now.

"The keys! I forgot the keys!" Sam plunged back up the stairs.

Here came the maid with Charles and Patty tucked under her arms. Raw heat roared on all sides, searing Susanna's naked body. Fire blotted out reason and sent dirty churning smoke into her eyes and lungs.

Sam was back, his key ring rattling. The yellow staircase exploded afire behind him. There would be no more going upstairs. Thank God the chambers and nursery were empty!

Where were the children? Susanna couldn't see. She could only feel the fire on all sides, pressing in, licking at her. She couldn't reach the garden door. Fire blocked the main door. And now Sam was beside her again, shielding her.

A tiny voice cried out from the nursery!

Susanna's heart thudded. "Sam! Jackie—!"

Sam turned to go back.

"No!" she screamed. "Don't!" but it was an idle request. The stairs, already aflame, shimmered and collapsed, howling, into a white-hot pile. Sparks splashed upward unrestricted to join the angry fire in the third floor.

Sobbing, Sam dropped to his knees and commended his son's soul to God.

How did Susanna get out? She didn't know. She remembered crying out to her Savior to help her. She remembered wading naked through open flame, and she ever remembered the cool, willing hands of neighbor women seizing her and wrapping her in aprons and petticoats. She was laid on a pallet of some sort in the chill grass.

Jackie! Her mystic, her devoted one, the child who most like her loved order and method in his young life. Then the boy's tiny head appeared in the second-floor nursery window, back lighted in bright yellow.

"Up there, lads!" cried a burly farmer. "On my back now, Billy! That's it." As the farmer braced himself against the stuccoed wall a quick slim little man clambered up onto his shoulders. The height of the two of them together just reached the bottom of the window. Jackie leaned out as the small man's hand grasped at his hair. The five-year-old came tumbling over the sill, safe in the arms of these unlettered servants of God. His feet were running as he touched ground, straight for Mama.

Even as those two wonderful men dashed away, the roof with a mighty howl dropped into the third-floor room. Roaring, the whole third floor collapsed into the second. Moments later the east wall caved inward slowly, casually, majestically. The north wall dipped a shoulder toward its fallen mate and just as nonchalantly crumpled into the thunderous blaze. Susanna's world melted in white heat.

There would be no saving anything this time, not books or notes or the twenty pounds cash tucked away in a desk drawer in the study. So much money— Those wonderful, musty old books—

Susanna had spent months writing a devotional manual for her children. It was gone, all gone, dissolved to nothing like hay and stubble. She mustn't let this devastating loss or the horror of the night affect her as it might. She mustn't let the terror and upset bring her unborn child into the world untimely. She must present a firm and staunch example to her children. And yet, this hurt so. Something seemed to reach in and snatch her heart right out of her.

No one bothered to fight the fire. The blaze had won, hands down. The other two walls fell. People moved back and shielded their faces from the heat. Sparks and brands danced like a million demons through the night sky. Neighbors were lifting her, pallet and all, to carry her to the Wilkes house next door. Sam and the other children would be there.

And Jackie would be there, miraculously plucked from sure destruction at the last possible moment. She vowed to God right there to pay special care to this little soul God had so mercifully provided for. It was clear God had special plans for little Jackie. Susanna's job was clear as well—to rear the child in the fear and nurture of the Lord and train him both in letters and behavior to be pleasing to God, useful to God.

Safe. No prodigal, little Jackie, yet the word Susanna had quoted once regarding Sammy when he had been lost pertained even more so. Scripture always served well. *For this my son was dead and is alive again, was lost and is found.*

13

A Chance to Serve

When a person feels bright and cheerful, she hardly needs further cheering. And when she feels morbidly, grindingly melancholy, the last thing in the world she wants to hear is some grinning cricket chirping, "Cheer up!" in her ear.

Sam the cricket was coming. She could hear his horse cantering from five doors up the street and knew it was he without looking. She thought briefly of the day when she identified the post horse, her link then to the man of her dreams.

She pushed out through the garden gate—it ought to be repainted, for it had blistered in the fire—and shifted baby Kezia from one hip to the other. She stepped across broken bricks and bats, around the accoutrements of construction so carelessly scattered through her yard, and barely glanced at the old oak tree. After all those centuries of survival it had succumbed to the heat of a senseless fire; the very thought made her sadder still. She met Sam as he dismounted out front.

He flashed her one of his ceaseless smiles and squeezed her shoulders. "Made a purchase today. A surprise for you."

"Really." This would be a perfect opportunity to mention their indebtedness, but she would refrain. Such nagging did no good; Sam would always be a spendthrift whether she threw it up to him or not.

Sam cranked his head upward to watch the masons at their trade capping the new chimney. "Beautiful! Just beautiful, isn't it! All brick. No more half-timbered tinderbox. Future rectors will thank us."

Perhaps she'd mention indebtedness after all. "It'd better be beautiful, to sink us four hundred pounds deeper in the mire."

"Eh, no, luv!" Sam gave her another squeeze. "More surprises for you. You remember John Sheffield."

"Marquis of Normanby. Of course." Bitter memories concerning their differences over the unfortunate widow came flooding back.

"He's Duke of Buckingham now. And he just contributed a hefty sum toward the four hundred it's costing to replace this manse. We're not nearly as deep in the mire as you thought." He guided her by the shoulders back to the blistered garden gate. They stood a few moments. She wished they'd go elsewhere. The garden no longer lifted her spirits.

He studied brown patches and green. "You were right. We lost some of the herbs closest the house. I'm glad to see your sweetbrier came through all green and healthy."

"That gnarled oak is gone, though. And I doubt the one apple tree will live—this one that the fire forced into bloom so early. Look at the leaves. All brown around the edges. And no apples this year. Not one."

"We have the other apple trees, and the pears. And also—" Sam took a deep breath. "No, I'll wait."

"My surprise." Why didn't she feel more anticipation? She didn't care, that's why. She didn't care about anything lately.

"Yes. And I've hired the Grimes boy—not the little one, the older one—as a sort of yard hand around the place. He'll keep the gardening up, tend the animals, handle all the outside work. We've long needed someone for that."

There went the prospect of another inside maid. They couldn't afford one domestic, let alone three.

Jackie came boiling into the yard at a dead run. He wrapped himself around his Papa—his standard greeting—and opened up with uncharacteristic enthusiasm. "Ye shoulda seen old Sweeney just now! He was riding that new gelding of his up Side Street—his real antsy little horse, y'know—and one of Jase Hooker's brothers whistled. I mean loud! That horse jumped straight up and come down running, and old Sweeney went straight up with it but when he came straight down the horse weren't under him anymore, and you shoulda seen him light in the dirt! It was funny! Jase and me, we laughed till—" and the eager soprano trailed away to silence. Jackie was staring at his mother.

Susanna stared aghast at him.

Jackie shrugged self-consciously. "Well, it was kind of funny. If you were there and saw it."

Shocked, Susanna held her tongue a few moments to marshal her complaints into some sort of order. "You know the difference between good English and careless English, and you will not use careless speech. Never! You do not refer to that gentleman as 'old' Sweeney. You address him respectfully and refer to him respectfully. And most of all, you never ever laugh at such a painful misfortune in another soul. There is and was nothing funny about it." Her voice rose. "Do you understand?"

"Yes'm." Jackie looked near tears, and well he should! Where had he dumped the politeness and good deportment she had drilled into him since infancy?

"Well, now, perhaps it's not as bad as all that." Sam was going to let the boy off again. Susanna would have none of it.

She cut him off. "It's worse than all that! Not only is the boy being corrupted, I don't even have a room to send him to as punishment! Sam, we must get that house finished and get these children back under our roof! We *must!* All the good manners and civility I've tried to instill in them have disappeared just as surely as if they'd burned in the fire as well!"

Sam dipped his head toward Jackie. "Go to your place, lad."

Jackie scampered off toward the Hookers'.

"Unlettered, uncultured bumpkins with filthy mouths and the manners of a plow ox. Sam—your children—" She sagged against him, utterly spent.

"It was an unlettered, uncultured bumpkin who served as God's instrument in saving him from the fire, you know." But Sam didn't sound chiding. "I'll talk to the builder about putting on extra men—get the house done quicker. I worry about you, Sukey. Every misfortune past, you bounced back, so to speak. This latest one seems to have buried you. It's as if you never quite recovered from either the fire or the childbirth." His voice dropped. "And I don't know how to help you."

"I don't know how to help me either. Nothing matters anymore. I don't care if I eat or starve, live or die, nothing. I can't even seem to warm up my feelings toward you, but you certainly haven't changed in any way. It's all so—" Words, so long her friends, failed her utterly. Her tongue stumbled momentarily and gave up. The bitter, empty feeling that dragged down her heart and soul refused to reduce itself to spoken words.

His huge warm hand pressed her head against his shoulder, the blunt fingertips gently massaging her temple. She had petitioned God for respite and nothing had happened. Where was God when you needed Him?

Even before the new brick house was complete, Susanna began moving in. She purchased a small dining table, then traded with the Grimeses for their long one. With their boys leaving home one by one, they didn't need a long board anymore, and, counting tiny Kezzy, Susanna now served nine children at table. She obtained simple slab bedframes to serve until they could afford more substantial furniture. She ordered bookshelves built in what would eventually be the library although not a single book had survived the fire. Not one musty old book. The empty shelves depressed her further every time she looked at them.

She wrote long sad letters to Sammy in London, describing progress and lack of it. She bemoaned the loss of the papers that she had so carefully accumulated and of the little manual she had been compiling for years to help the children in their walk with God. One of her cows came fresh out of season, and a stoat got at their chickens with disastrous consequences.

And then, on some day or other that Susanna didn't really notice, life turned around again. Perhaps it was Sam's surprise for her that arrived one pleasant September afternoon. From Lincoln came a nurseryman in a sturdy wagon. Without so much as by-your-leave he parked his wagon by the garden gate, dragged his shovel out from under the seat, and unceremoniously planted mulberry trees!

Mulberry trees. For decades Susanna had dreamed of owning mulberry trees. Now here they stood, their leaves just a wee bit droopy, along the sunny side of her garden wall. The nurseryman warned her against expecting much fruit for a few years until the trees had established themselves, climbed over his wagon wheel, and drove away. Even more precious to Susanna than her lovely mulberry trees was the fact that Sam would remember her wish so many years after she had voiced it. How can you long remain upset with a spendthrift who spends to make you happy, in ways you would never have guessed?

The day finally came when she could again assemble her brood in a single nest. Sukey and Hetty, farmed out to their Uncle Matthew in London, returned home—gratefully, they said, but Susanna could clearly tell that they had enjoyed living the city life. Even those two girls, ages fourteen and twelve and (one should think) fairly responsible, had picked up irritating habits and mannerisms. Uncle Matthew was a much looser disciplinarian than Susanna had thought a doctor would be.

And the rest of her flock! Coarse jokes, silly stories, bad English, uncivil attitudes and behavior—the world had sown many weeds in Susanna's carefully nurtured garden, and it would surely cause her considerable difficulty to root them out. But reform her children she would.

As soon as the children had learned which new bed was theirs she gathered them in their new kitchen. She looked from face to uncertain face. "Most of you are too tender of years to recognize good from bad and better from good. It's my province to teach you the difference, and I shall.

"So that no one is slighted, we'll arrange the day according to a method, a schedule. Most of our rules you already know, but you seem to have forgotten them. If you confess a fault freely and don't try to cover it up you'll not be beaten for it. Once

161

you are punished for a fault it will not be mentioned again; our Lord fully forgives trespass and so shall I.

"No sinful actions, and you know what they are—lying, pilfering, and such. You'll keep any promise you make, even it it's to little Kezzy here, and you'll respect each others' property. No borrowing without permission, do you hear, Emilia? And if you give a gift, it's given forever, not until you want it back—unless you made that condition, of course."

She drew a long breath and looked about. What lovely children she had! They were worth every effort to raise well. She would assign a chapter of Old Testament in the morning and New in the evening, and psalms twice daily. Nothing equaled Scripture for teaching children—or adults, for that matter.

From then on each child from Jackie on up applied himself or herself to studies six hours daily. Older children helped tutor the younger ones. They sang psalms at the beginning and end of each school day. They began bedtime preparations at five, ate at six, held devotions privately at seven and were tucked away by eight. The household began to march to the stable routine Susanna so preferred.

"There is nothing I desire to live for but to do some small service to my children," she wrote to Sammy, "that as I've brought them into the world, I may, if it please God, be an instrument of doing good to their souls."

Either working the winter convocation or escaping routine—Susanna was never quite sure which—Sam went back to London. His occasional letters seemed as much concerned with finding sponsors for his poetry as for matters of convocation business. After a long dry spell of not caring, Susanna began to miss him.

The year 1710 came and went with no new baby. No objection there—Kezzy was babe enough, and for the first winter in years, Susanna was not bedridden. The new year brought other problems, though.

It started so innocently. The curate assigned to handle services in Sam's absence was paid forty pounds annually of the eighty pounds to which the living had shrunk. Curate Inman, with no family to support, generally preached on the necessity of paying one's debts. Rarely did two dozen people show up on a Sunday morning to listen to him.

Susanna as usual included the Grimes boy and her maid in the private Sunday evening service she held for her own children. The servant boy began bringing his parents. One thing led to another and before Susanna quite realized it, thirty or forty people crowded into her new brick home to hear Scripture and the short, simple message she prepared for her children.

The months ticked off, marching relentlessly in their expected formation. Spring brought smallpox. Jackie and four of his sisters nearly died. Sam came home for the summer and hied himself right back to London come winter.

With Sam gone and Pastor Inman preaching empty words to an empty house, Susanna took up her Sunday evening service again. She spent more time this year on preparation of prayers and messages, for her simple service for her children was, quite frankly, getting out of hand. Two hundred people crowded into the ground floor of the manse each Sunday night! And the maid turned uncounted others away.

"I really should refuse all these people admittance," she confided to Jackie, "but I don't feel I dare. They can't even read, most of them, and the curate never dwells at any length on Scripture. The only place they're likely to hear the pure Word is here."

But her arguments were not for Jackie's benefit; they were for her. Properly, only ordained men should offer up to God the prayers of the people, and she was neither. She had entered the province of men, usurping the duties of men. They were the pastors, preachers, lay readers. Women were instructed by Scripture to keep silence in the churches.

And yet, perversely, she felt a heady joy in this accidental role as leader of a service. Flocks of people, illiterate people unable to read Scripture for themselves, were hungry for the Word, and she could feed them. They looked up to her. They needed her. She could help them.

Sam wrote her a letter; he'd heard rumors about unseemly actions on her part that looked most peculiar. They weren't true, were they?

She remembered well the bitter fruit of that business with the marquis's widow, and frankly she was still convinced that Sam had been in the wrong. And that business with the Prince of Orange; again, Sam had taken a most obstreperous position. She had learned a thing or two from them. It would be very, very easy to tip Sam off into one of his adamant snits again. She must frame her response extremely carefully.

She pointed out that the responsibility for the children's spiritual instruction was Sam's, but since he wasn't home she must be the one to discharge it. She was merely attending to the same sort of evening devotions Sam had led. The other people coming was accidental, but how could she turn them away, after all?

She mentioned in passing that it wasn't really a party or social thing; they stuck to the business at hand, then went home. She couldn't see why anyone should object to all those people being drawn to Scripture instead of profaning the Lord's day as so many do.

He wrote back with the sort of half-in-water-half-on-land equivocal reply he made so well. If she would continue, at least find a male to do the reading. Obviously Sam had missed the crux of the whole problem. There *were* no men who could read well enough! The best male reader at the service was Jackie, and his soft soprano would never carry through the two rooms full of listeners.

A scant week later another letter arrived from Sam forbidding her to hold services. Curate Inman was worried, he said, because she was scandalously turning the house into a conventicle, and certain other parishioners agreed. She knew what was *really* worrying the curate: ten times more people attended her evening devotions than were showing up at church! Were she the inept curate, she'd be worried, too.

She must be *very* careful in her answer this time. If Sam maintained his position, as well he might, it would all be over. Why did she want so much to continue these Sunday evening sessions? Was it concern for her neighbors, whose unmannerly ways she tried so hard to erase from her children's behavior? Or was it Susanna Annesley Wesley's self, her ugly Adamic self, rearing its nasty head? She enjoyed it so—the respect of adults, being the center of quiet attention. She could command that sort of thing from her children just by the sheer force of being their mother. From the outside world, though, such respect came only when you earned it, and it pleased her immensely that these people thought enough of her devotionals to come. The more she explored her motives during meditation and devotions, the more confused she got.

Very well, motives aside, teaching Scripture to the village folk was a good thing—a thing God must surely approve under any circumstance. She would not let a good thing slip away easily just because a frightened and jealous curate wrote letters to a rector who didn't really know what was happening.

She took pen in hand and began to write.

166

"I shall not inquire," she began, "how it was possible that you should be prevailed on by the senseless clamors of two or three of the worst of your parish to condemn what you so lately approved."

So far, so good. She had best list next the good that came from these meetings. Constant attention to public worship, for example, because many of those attending never set foot inside the steeple-building. She also mentioned in detail the way these meetings had altered people's attitudes toward the Tory rector and his ministry: "We live in the greatest amity imaginable," she wrote. That was not far from the truth, for she had not for years fooled herself into imagining any good feelings at all from the locals.

She took the bull by the horns, so to speak, in her ending. She asked for his positive command if he still insisted she quit, for no weaker expression of his wishes would satisfy her conscience. Was that too strong? She rewrote it several times and ended up with her original wording. With some trepidation and much prayer she sent it off by post.

Whatever she said worked. No positive command came thundering into Lincolnshire Wolds from London. Susanna put her mounting doubts behind her, and gradually they ebbed. If God decreed that she, a lowly female, should by happenstance find herself in this position, she would fill it. Her services continued successfully all through the winter as the nervous curate fidgeted and fussed.

Come spring when Rector Sam Wesley returned to his parish of St. Andrews, he found himself preaching Sundays to a full house.

In amity.

14

Saturday's Child

Emilia was so pretty. Barely into her twenties, she combined the bloom of youth with gentle maturity—the perfect age. Versed in child care, too, and responsible, she would be a fine catch for some lucky young man—should any lucky young man happen by and notice her. Emilia might as well be living in a convent, so cloistered her household and so bleak the male prospects in Epworth outside it.

Susanna shifted slightly in her chair and leaned back, eyes closed, as Emilia's voice floated along. Susanna enjoyed this time of day just about best. Emilia liked to read aloud, and Susanna appreciated the chance to rest her tired eyes and let her ears do the work. With Sam gone again, it was just the two of them once the maid and younger children were off to bed. Mother and daughter, teacher and student, and now, friend and friend.

"The End." Emilia closed the book. "That was better than I thought it would be. Two Danish missionaries in Tranquebar sounds a bit dull until you get into it. Considering all that happened to them, and how aware they were that those difficulties would be there, I can't understand why they went in the first place."

"They didn't go, Em. They were sent. Great difference."

"God would send them deliberately into such hardship? What kind of goodness is that?"

Susanna perked upright. "Divine goodness. You just read an account of two Danes, from their point of view. Consider God's point of view. He cares for those two men He sent and also, as much, for the lost souls in that remote outpost. The missionaries suffered hardship in order to do God's will, not just in themselves but for the lost. Don't you see?"

Emilia shrugged. "I know the two Danes bought themselves a lot of treasure in heaven." Then she corrected herself hastily. "I understand that's not why they did it; I don't mean that."

"I understand. Yes, I agree with you." Susanna melted back again into her soft chair. "I often wonder if there is something more I can do for the glory of God."

"I can't believe you of all people would say that! You serve Him every day, from morning prayer through school and devotions right to now."

"That's as much for me as for Him. It's how I draw strength. I mean something just for Him."

"Mama—" Emilia's voice was so tight, so earnest, that Susanna opened her eyes to watch her. "Mama, you don't realize how it hurts us when Papa's gone so much. He chases after money that isn't there while he spends money that isn't there either. He spends all his time at home on that poetry of his that no one reads, and then he spends all his spare time away trying to get someone to buy it."

"He's a man of faith, Emilia. His religion is pure, and that covers a lot of faults."

"Sure. Covers a lot of faults. But it doesn't help Jackie, who's pretty much grown up without a father. It doesn't help Charles who doesn't really know who the man is. And us girls—we—" Emilia sighed and sagged back. "It's bitter with him gone. That's all I can say. I resent him leaving you to raise his children all alone. And I resent that we never have enough money for simple things. Decent clothes, books to read—anything."

"I never realized how strongly you felt."

"Ever since I've been old enough to help with the house. Until I had to go out and find bread and then scrape some little bit together to pay for it, I didn't realize how hard it was to keep this family going, and I hate it. I hate the haggling."

Susanna's memory blurred back to Southwark and her sister Elizabeth's haggling—and how Susanna hated the haggling and in her wide-eyed innocence had vowed never to stoop to that. And now, her own daughter— "Society offers no opportunity for intelligence in its women, but you might be able to marry out of it."

171

"Not sitting here."

"No. Not sitting here." Susanna pondered a few minutes and detested the conclusions her mind kept drawing. "We've neglected you, Emilia, your father and I. I'll write to him instantly and tell him to look for a position for you, and you and I will seek one also. You're very well educated. You can teach. We'll get you out someplace where you can meet a good man."

Emilia laughed. "Is finding me a husband your extra service to the glory of God?"

Susanna smiled. "Of course." The smile faded. "No, I want to do more. Charles is four, not really ready for serious thought about any topic he can't see with his eyes. Same with Kezzy, who's three. But the rest of you—know what I want to do? For the glory of God start right here, with my own children. Give each of you an hour of my time, just to yourselves. No interference, no other children. One each evening. We'll squeeze some time in after supper."

"You mean like Monday is Molly's and Tuesday is Hetty's and that?"

"Yes. What do you think?"

"Monday's child is fair of face; Tuesday's child is full of grace; Wednesday's child is full of woe; Thursday's child has far to go; Friday's child is loving and giving; Saturday's child works hard for a living. But the child that's born on the Sabbath day is blithe and winsome and bonny and gay."

"Where did you get that?"

"Hester down the road, when I stayed with her after the fire."

172

Susanna wagged her head. "Years later, and you children still remember all those paganish bits of trash, when you can't recall how to decline a Greek verb decently."

"We're certainly not so naive as to believe such things; it's just a verse to say." Emilia blew out her candle and shelved the book. She headed for the stairs. "Good night, Mama."

"Good night, dear."

She paused at the stairs. "Mama? What day was I born on?"

Those two Danish missionaries could never have dreamed that the story of their work would prompt a mother to give her nine-year-old Jackie an hour each Thursday. Susanna had precious little time to meditate on the way one's works influence others in mysterious and far-flung ways; she was too busy entertaining doubts. Could she spare the time? What would she talk about with just one child, for the children were all totally accustomed to operating in the midst of a big friendly group?

Monday, Mary. Sixteen and full of life, Molly seemed to be handling her deformity well by ignoring it. Susanna learned to her mild surprise that the child planned marriage and family just as much as any other girl, and she seemed to have the right notions about what to seek in a husband.

Tuesday, Mehetabel. Hetty Wesley was the mischievous one, the wild one, the romantic. She pictured knights on white horses, as well she might at fifteen. So had Susanna at fifteen.

Wednesday, Anne. Ten-year-old Nancy on first appearance seemed dull and listless. Susanna at last got to know the girl beneath the surface and learned quickly to appreciate her gentle, quiet, methodical way of thinking.

Thursday, John. Jackie. Her brand plucked from the fire. Quick and clever in some ways, plodding and taciturn in so many others; he was utterly unlike Sammy at nine or any of the girls at any age.

Friday, Martha. Patty was only five. For the first time since Sammy's infancy Susanna could enjoy a small child. Through Patty she learned how many little things she had missed in the other children as baby came upon baby.

Saturday ended up becoming Charles's day. He seemed the sort never to outgrow his childish impetuosity, so like his father. Even before he could read and cipher he blotted up not just knowledge but ingenious ways to put that knowledge to unusual use.

Sundays Susanna devoted an hour each to Emilia and Sukey. Like so many of her projects intended to give glory to God, such as home services, this too satisfied her as much as it served her Lord. Her doubts about what to do for an hour evaporated. The difficulty became to crowd into a limited time all that both wanted to talk about.

And she began again to prepare religious texts for the children's use. She assembled a commentary on the Apostles' Creed to give them insight into the liturgy. She built a similar exposition on the Ten Commandments. Her study, all poured

174

into her head, was beginning to pour back out, and it gave her a solid feeling of satisfaction.

With Sammy years gone to school, Susanna pictured her maturing daughters as the next to leave the nest. She was shocked when in 1714 Sam and Sammy got Jackie placed in the Charterhouse preparatory school, with an eye toward Oxford. How could they do that? The lad was her little man at home, not even twelve yet.

At age twenty-five Sammy decided on a girl he loved and married in London. Not only was the boy bright and studious, he possessed all Sam's virtues and few of Sam's faults. Sammy's poetry received a wider acceptance than his father's ever had. And Sammy could handle money. From the age of seventeen on he sent Susanna money regularly to help support brothers and sisters he had never even seen.

A year later in 1716 they spirited Charles away just as they had robbed her of Jackie. At the age of eight Charles left her nurturing, tutoring, disciplining, molding—much too early to be deprived of a mother's strong influence. Susanna felt cruelly betrayed by men in general and her men in particular. She knew it was un-Christian, and yet she couldn't scrub that feeling out of her thoughts no matter how hard she tried.

Sukey married a lout named Dick Ellison simply to get away from the poverty. Susanna was bitterly disappointed in her choice. She really shouldn't have let it show, but it probably did. Sam, never one to hide opinions, started calling

Dick the wen of the family, and a painful cyst the fellow was, too.

Emilia found a position teaching in Gainsborough and, with money from Uncle Matthew and her brothers, eventually opened her own school. She struggled so desperately, Susanna ached for her.

Nancy married timely, a gentle and rather pedestrian young man named Lambert. They suited each other perfectly.

Susanna awoke one morning to realize how rapidly her flock was shrinking. She thought of her own mother's brood diminishing as one girl then another married, one boy then another went out into the world to seek his fortune—and hardly ever found it. And now it was Susanna's turn.

But one boy had found it. Her brother Sam, the genius of the family, had built himself a personal fortune in trade with the East India Company. And in 1724 Samuel determined to return to England from his home abroad, bringing his wealth. Susanna was a fifty-five year old woman who hadn't borne a child in fourteen years. Affairs around the house could attend themselves for once. For the first time in thirty-five years Susanna would go home and greet her brother.

The fact that she had not actually been bed-ridden for some years had masked the fact that she was not a strong woman. The one-hundred-fifty mile journey wearied her greatly. She resisted the compelling mother-urge to hasten straight to Westminster and hug her Sammy and Charles. Instead she rode directly down to the docks at Billingsgate.

The dock and the market here were exactly as she remembered them. The odor of stale water and aging fish still pervaded the riverfront. The same shrill voices hawked slabs of salt cod that looked exactly as it had thirty-five years ago.

Little bobbing smacks rubbed shoulders with stately galleons as fishermen and tradesmen came and went. Two men here complained about the risky channel between the starlings of London Bridge. Over there three others were heatedly denouncing the flat market in squid and mussels. Fishwives outshouted everybody in their eagerness to sell their slimy merchandise.

Nothing here had changed, and for a shining moment this churning, bustling scene rejuvenated her. It brought back to life dormant memories of youth and vitality, when she prowled these docks for bargains and haggled with the best of them.

That must be Samuel's ship out there, that great yellowish bulk of a vessel with most of its sails furled. It ghosted on a gentle breeze, pushing slowly and casually up the main channel at the speed of a strolling man. Susanna walked along the shore beside it, shouldering through clusters of conversationalists and loiterers, sidestepping pushcarts.

The East Indiaman turned majestically; the sail slung below its jib flapped; then it slipped sideways ever so slowly and bumped casually against the wharf. Men shouted as they tossed about ropes thicker around than Susanna's waist. Her heart began to thump in anticipation.

Heads clustered beyond the railing amid ships as seamen threw out a gangplank; it thudded against the stone-and-timber quay. Here came several men, at least one of them a passenger. Susanna worked her way in closer to the foot of the gangplank.

That wasn't him. Nor was that—nor that fellow. An uneasy trill bothered her stomach and began inching up her breastbone. Where was Samuel? She waited a respectable time after the last departee, then marched up the steep gangway. For the first time in her life she set her foot upon a cambered deck. She noted in passing that it was quite as stable as solid land and walked over to the first man she saw.

"Excuse me. I'm seeking out a passenger, Samuel Annesley."

The man barely glanced at her. "Annesley? Eh, nae, mum." He turned immediately back to his work of coiling a coarse rope.

"Who might know him here?"

"Ye could ask aft, I s'pose."

"Thank you." She hesitated. "Which way is aft?"

The man waved an arm toward the rear of the vessel.

She was quite clearly in the way here. Seamen and dock hands were bringing all manner of crates and bales up from below. The deck was already stacked high; Susanna barely found room to slip past the cargo and the shouting, sweaty workmen.

The sterncastle rose at a majestic slant, all gaudy with its intricate carving and bright colors.

178

Its paneled door was every bit as elaborate as the great oaken doors of St. Mark's. The ornate outside piqued her curiosity to see the interior, but she didn't get the opportunity.

A somber magisterial sort came stepping out of the door. He paused and squinted as his crinkly eyes adjusted to the light.

"Excuse me. Are you in charge?"

The man studied her. "I'm her master, aye."

"I'm here to meet my brother Samuel Annesley, a passenger."

"Nae, mum, not aboard this vessel."

"I can read, sir, and your trailboards attest that this is his ship. From the Spice Islands. Annesley; about sixty-five, well dressed, well-spoken, eyes and hair similar to mine."

He stared at her for the longest time. She felt an anxiety welling up in her, and it came as much from this man's gaze as from the situation. "I'm sorry, mum."

"I'd like to see your passenger manifest, please."

His demeanor shifted, hardened. "As ye wish. Y'll find him at the beginning of it but not the end. He took quite ill early on and was by his own request put ashore. It's in the log."

"And his effects? His baggage?"

"With him, mum, wherever he be now."

She wanted to argue further, somehow reverse this nightmare, but nothing she could say would change this man's story. She mumbled something about returning and squeezed past the growing mountain of things on deck. She fell in between two porters and walked the gangway to solid ground.

Who could help her? The crown maintained an investigating board and full court to handle maritime affairs. Sammy would know where to go, whom to see. Sam might also, although he wasn't very good at business matters.

In the end she received no satisfaction. Neither Samuel nor the fortune he was purportedly bringing home could be traced. Even though the authorities agreed the circumstances were suspicious, they also agreed that they could do nothing.

Susanna visited in London awhile, reacquainting herself with the sights and smells of yesteryear. She went to see St. Paul's Cathedral just for curiosity; it had been started about the time she was born and finally completed fourteen years ago.

And then she journeyed home to shabby, muddy parochial little Epworth, strangely empty-hearted.

15

Wednesday's Children

The weather out of Lincolnshire's skies usually consists of long spates of clouds and rain broken by occasional sunshine. The sunshine was good for the soul and for the rosemary mounded against the garden wall, the frequent rain good for flowers and herbs. And Susanna found her life going pretty much the same way.

The bit of sunshine was Jackie, who in 1726 became a fellow in Lincoln at age twenty-three. Susanna was proud that her son had persevered so diligently in his studies and service to God, even though his way had been hard. Sam was proud because his son had achieved the elevated status of fellow.

Otherwise, including the matter of Samuel's tragic disappearance, clouds crowded out the blue sky and rained on her.

At fifteen Kezzy went away to Mrs. Taylor's seminary, which in itself was good. Susannah now had time to study and read—but no money for books! She prevailed in vain upon Sam to somehow find some.

Patty traveled to London to live with Uncle Matthew the doctor and there met a clergy student named Westley Hall. Sam optimistically assumed the relationship was like that between himself and his Sukey so many years before. Susanna, of a more practical viewpoint, was pretty sure it wasn't.

Sam took a living at Wroote, five miles across the marsh, in addition to his living at Epworth. Together the two positions brought in about half the income the Epworth living used to twenty years before. Sam rented out their warm, tight brick house and moved what was left of his family to a damp cottage on the edge of a town even smaller and meaner than South Ormsby. From this new base he served the tiny Wroote church. When bad weather made the road impassable he was forced to row a boat across the marsh weekly to deliver eucharist and services in Epworth.

Hetty found the man of her dreams, she said. Susanna called him the man of her nightmares. She and Sam, who so rarely agreed on anything, could both see through the bounder. Why couldn't her daughter see that the cad was a smooth-talking womanizer? To Sam's shock and Susanna's dismay, Hetty ran off with her lawyer knight, later to return when he refused to marry her.

"'Tis an unhappiness almost peculiar to our family," Susanna wrote to Jackie, "that your father and I seldom think alike." They thought alike on this issue, though. When it was apparent that

Hetty was pregnant, Sam married her to what was essentially the first man down the pike. The abandoned mother-to-be became Mrs. Will Wright, bride of a journeyman plumber from Lincoln.

Sam disowned the girl, but Susanna felt more than that. Betrayed. She was betrayed by a girl she had tried so hard to raise and nurture in the faith.

In a way, Susanna even felt betrayed by God. She had lived her life His way. She had written to her sons, "What creature under heaven, that has the use of reason, can be ignorant of the being of God, and that they ought to live in subjection to him from whom they receive their own being?" She had reared her children to know and revere Him. And now this. How could He let this happen when Susanna was playing correctly, by the rules?

Life at home got worse. Like all Sam's money-making schemes, rental of the Epworth manse cost more than it brought in. Finally Sam moved his family back to Epworth.

And Sam began his magnum opus, a dissertation on the book of Job—in Latin. Every child at home or who came home to visit ended up in his study helping with notes. When the children finally rebelled, he brought in a local boy with promise, a Johnny Whitelamb.

Molly's dream of so many years, to marry like any other girl, finally came true. John Whitelamb loved her so much he didn't notice her crippling. The little ray of sunshine, the little strip of blue in Susanna's cloudy sky, lasted less than a year. Molly, so happily married, died in childbirth. The baby died, too.

In November of 1731 Sukey almost died in childbirth. Susanna went to her, contracted pleurisy, and nearly died herself. The burden of Hetty's grief came back upon her as if it were fresh. Molly's death, so cruel; Sam's inattention, cruel in its own way; the years of debt that hadn't eased a shilling; Sukey's bad marriage; they weighed Susanna down to the pits of hell. Come February she was still in bed. And she didn't care.

More than thirty years of struggle, and here she lay without a spare farthing. She vowed to offer herself absolutely and entirely if it please God to give food and raiment without debt, without this extreme distress. And even as she uttered the vow she held scant hope God would listen.

A philanthropist named James Oglethorpe proposed a settlement in the New World to be colonized out of the debtors' prisons. The man reasoned that if these luckless fellows had a fresh start and no debt burden they would become useful, successful citizens of the realm. Sam signed up; if anyone qualified as a debtor, he did.

Susanna didn't gainsay him; it would have done no good; but she knew better than to dream that Sam would ever get ahead of his debts, not even in the New World with so far fewer places to spend money. Sam finally decided he was too old and canceled his application.

He was becoming too old to handle the Wroote living and had to give it up. He fell from the wagon during a ride in the country, to all appearances dead, yet managed to celebrate the eucharist come Sunday two days later. His right hand, though, was left so paralyzed he had to learn to write with his left.

Westley Hall and Patty spent the winter of '33 at Epworth. Wes threw Patty over for Kezzy, who at twenty-three was one of the prettiest of the seven Wesley girls. Whatever happened in that messy triangle Susanna never clearly learned. Wes went back to Patty and married her, took up a living in London, and invited Kezzy to live with them there.

How Kezzy could take part in such a thing she didn't know. But nothing the girls would do could shock her anymore, it seemed. This was simply additional chickens coming home to roost—her fault in not exposing her girls more to life and to the world out there.

Emilia at age forty-four found a half-way decent man and settled for him. She was so tired of working, so wearied of the struggle to keep her school going. She wanted a man to care for her and let her be simply a wife and mother. But her Robert Harper, unbeknownst to her, was tired of working too and wearied of the struggle to earn his living. He wanted simply to be kept by a successful woman so he wouldn't have to work. He took her savings and left her, eventually, with a sickly, dying baby and his debts.

Then the thing Susanna dreaded most came creeping up upon her to turn her cloudy days to absolute night. Sam began to slip. First he had trouble writing with either hand. Then his coordination deteriorated until celebrating eucharist was difficult for him. His mind drifted. By 1735 he was confined to bed.

He claimed to want only three things—be out of debt, to see his Job dissertation in print, and to die with Sammy at his side.

None of them was happening.

To Susanna life suddenly appeared futile. Serving God must be its own reward, for she saw no other. Every time she entered Sam's sickroom her legs turned to water. She had known for years this would happen. But now that Sam's time was here, she couldn't stand it. Faults forgotten, he was her love.

And yet, just as in the beginning Susanna's practicality was tempered by Sam's optimism, so it was even yet, forty-six years after their wedding. Susanna saw death standing at the head of Sam's bed while to the very end Sam saw revival blossoming out of Epworth.

Although Sammy couldn't get away from his responsibilities, Jackie and Charles came home. They were holding Sam's hands when he died.

The week following, somehow, seemed a bit easier than the weeks preceding. At least now the outcome was certain. Sam was in glory, and Susanna wrote his epitaph. She handled his passing much more calmly than she would have thought she could.

The boys sold off all the rusting farm tools, the cows and chickens, the current pig. Except for a few stray pieces, the house was emptied of furnishings. The new rector would furnish it. Susanna would live at Gainsborough with Emilia.

Two of Sam's wishes in life finally saw fruit; the debt was, after a lifetime plaguing Susanna, at last discharged. And the dissertation on Job in Latin saw print. Even in death, Sam's confidence remained ill placed. He had envisioned his dissertation as the crowning achievement of his life, to be welcomed by an admiring world, to be the instrument to lift him out of debt and put him in the ranks of Britain's great scholars. It sold less than five hundred copies.

According to his desire a copy was given to Queen Caroline, in hopes that a generous stipend might be forthcoming, reflective of its worth.

She liked the binding.

16

Sweetbrier

The last day of May. Too early for the sweetbrier to bloom. Susanna strolled down the lane beyond Westley and Patty's little vicarage to admire
this clump of sweetbrier growing along a mossy
stone wall. Sam had died three years ago plus a
month. Susanna still wasn't quite prepared for his
death. Strange how the man had captured her spirit, despite all the separations and bitter disagree-
ments, all the debts and neglect. Here she was
nearly seventy, and she still had no idea of the
strength and depth of true love.

The post was coming. Here the carrier came
up off the glen and around the bend. He drew nigh
and stopped.

"Mrs. Wesley, g'day! Letter for ye." He riffled
in a sack draped across his saddle. "Some'eres." He
grinned. The man truly delighted in mail. "Y'r son
Jackie, mum."

"Thank you. Care to save me the trouble of opening it by telling me his news?"

"Nae, mum, I'd never read mail. 'Tis agin' the crown's rules." He reined his horse away, then drew it in again. "Who's the Moravians or whatever, mum?"

"The modern version of John Huss's Brethren, stressing Scripture and simplicity in worship. Their headquarters is Herrnhut in Saxony."

"Mm. You and y'r boys—y'r daughter here, too—y're all so marvelous smart. Ye know so much."

"I know about the Moravians because Jackie was associated with them on his trip to America."

"Y'r son went to the colonies?" The man's eyes spread wide with wonder. "Coo, mum!"

"Two sons, Jackie and Charles. Missionaries to the Indians. They left within weeks of—" her voice caught "—of my husband's death. They said they were afraid to leave me so soon after—that, but I was fine with Emilia. As I told them, if I had twenty sons I'd rejoice they were so employed, even if I never saw them again. I did, of course. Charles stayed in the New World a year and John two years. Oglethorpe's Georgia."

"Come back here to preach to us British heathens instead of them Indianish heathens." The man cackled.

"Exactly so. Do you still care to say we're all smart?"

"Eh, yea, mum." The grin soared again. "I appreciates smart people who sends lots of mail." Away he went.

A letter from Jackie. Delightful. She would read it now, on her ambling walk back to the vicarage, with the sweet smell of the damp meadow grass hovering around her.

In his measured prose, so stilted compared to the way he naturally spoke, he was describing a Moravian meeting he attended in Aldersgate Street. He even gave the exact time, 8:45 on the evening of May 24. Less than a week ago—he must have written her immediately thereafter.

"I felt I did trust in Christ, Christ alone for salvation; and an assurance was given me that he had taken away MY sins, even MINE, and saved ME from the law of sin and death."

Her feet stopped walking as her muddled head sorted this out. Of course Christ is responsible for salvation. Scripture said so. He knew she knew, and he knew she knew he knew. This must mean far more than just the theological truth everyone knew. He felt he trusted Christ. Felt. *Felt.* Not just head knowledge. Her Jackie was talking about an emotional experience of some sort, an aspect of the faith beyond the strictly rational.

This couldn't be the inner witness Sam used to talk about. Jackie surely would have used that term. She read happily that he would be stopping by on his way to Germany in early June.

Happily? That was relative. She was, true, finally getting over the numbing loss. Still she suffered the depths of melancholia that tended to hit her hard every couple of years. But then grief and shock—something concerning Sam or the children—tended to hit her hard every couple of years, too.

Countering the melancholia was her new freedom from debt. How she basked in her freedom from debt! God had made good His part in her vow made years ago. Now how could she give herself over to Him more completely?

By the time Jackie was due to arrive, the sweetbrier had cautiously offered forth its first buds. Susanna had to press very close to smell anything yet, though, for its overwhelming redolence was still several weeks away. She happened to be out walking along the lane when Jackie came in.

He still rode that sorry bay cob, and his appearance hadn't changed for years. Whereas most men, including Sammy, now wore carefully powdered wigs, those elaborate coats called fracs, and the new sort of britches, Jackie shunned fashion and parted his dark hair in the middle to let it tumble down over each ear. At thirty-five he still sported his mama's thin features and slim build.

With a happy grin Jackie slid off his plug and engulfed Susanna in a warm and satisfying hug. Her feet left the ground. "Hello, dear Mama."

"Put me down, please. How is my favorite son?"

"Doing well in Westminster. He sends his love."

She poked him. "You know what I mean."

His eyes danced. Was there a special air about him, a new enthusiasm? "Mama, we all know Sammy's your apple. Charles and I are happy and honored to be pears."

"Get on now!" She started slowly back the lane, relishing this moment alone with him. His arm encircled her shoulder as Sam's once had and drew her in close.

"Actually, you boys are perceptive. Sammy has been favored, I admit it. Sam treated him as the male firstborn, and his namesake. But I'm guilty, too. I love Sammy too well."

"Love too well? Can't be done."

"But I love you and Charles equally, in a different way. You are my brand plucked from the fire, my studious one, the one who appreciates method and order as I do. Charles is my little Sam, with so much of his father in him. You've all three served God faithfully. I'm so proud of you."

"You'd be surprised how much Charles enjoys method, too. Did he ever tell you about the Holy Club?"

"He doesn't write much. You've mentioned it."

"That prayer-and-study club Charles started at Oxford. I was in it for years, too. Some of the less reverent got to calling us methodists, because we ordered our life according to a method." His warm arm squeezed her. "Guess where we got *that*."

Susanna chuckled. "Years and years ago Emilia and I read an account of two Danish missionaries in—now where was that? Trans—no, Tranquebar. Thinking about that account got me wondering how I might serve God better, and one of the firstfruits was the hour each I spent with you children. I pondered then how a person's life causes ripples in others' lives in ways and at times that person could hardly imagine."

"Amazing when you think about it. Moravians a continent away go to another continent an ocean away and there influence me to greater piety here in London. Charles and I've had great success evangelizing in the country over this last summer."

"I heard. England's a better place for you two—and heaven richer in souls." How should she ask this? "You mentioned a special experience in your letter. Has Charles experienced it also?"

"Three days before me. He read Martin Luther's commentary on Galatians and underwent exactly the same sort of thing—a knowledge of salvation beyond reason."

"Indeed!" She stopped and turned to him. "That's the very same treatise that led to John Bunyan's saving insight; I read an account of the man's life some time ago, about the same time I read his Pilgrim's Progress." She turned and resumed walking. "You said in your letter your heart was strangely warmed."

"Inadequately phrased, but the closest I could come."

In all her sixty-nine years of service to her unseen God, Susanna's heart had never been warmed. It crouched chilled in her breast right now, victimized by her persistent melancholia. And since Sam's death it seemed to be getting colder.

"Mama, are you ready for eternity?"

"I believe so. I've reconciled myself to the past, all of it. I've even made peace with Hetty finally, after all those years. Forgave her and was forgiven by her."

"There is more, Mama, so much more. Here's the house. We'll talk again later."

Over the next few months Susanna became involved in a blizzard of letter-writing. Jackie read her a paper he had prepared about his new experience. It sounded good.

Sammy sent a paper to her he claimed was "brother John's" latest theology. The doctrinal errors so horrified her that she wrote to Jackie at Herrnhut asking him to come back and redress his wrongs—at any rate to set Sammy's heart at ease in the matter.

She wrote to Charles about her joy that he had found a deeper and renewed faith. He wrote a rare letter suggesting that he had had no spiritual life before this latest experience. She wrote back setting him straight on that matter; of course he had a spiritual life before this year—and a fruitful one!

By March of the next year Sammy had sent her enough material about Jackie's claims and his new friends that she was absolutely certain Jackie was subverting sound doctrine. She studied and fretted for weeks trying to sort out this swirl of theology that conflicted so with her mother-instinct and her native trust in Jackie's wisdom. Surely the boy couldn't be that far off the track, and yet Sammy was more mature in the faith, a good solid churchman with a good solid position.

Jackie and Charles had no positions, no livings, no churches to call their own, and that bothered Susanna. If their preaching in London and about was so good, as she heard, why didn't they work out of a church? It was the way things were done.

A gentleman named George Whitefield, an associate of Jackie's, was coming through Devon. He stopped by to meet Susanna and talk for a short while about Jackie's ministry.

George Whitefield had hardly left her presence before she began a letter to Sammy. "I told him I did not like their way of living, wished them in some place of their own, wherein they might regularly preach. He said I could not conceive the good they were doing in London, that the greater part of the clergy were asleep and there was never a greater need for itinerant preachers. Upon which a gentleman who came with him said my son Charles had converted him and that my sons spent all their time doing good. Then I asked him if my sons were not for making innovations in the church, which I fear. He assured me they were far from it."

She knew Sammy severely disapproved of the way his little brothers were approaching religion. The rift between brothers was a rift within the mother. Why could a woman not simply fledge her nestlings and put them behind her, the way rooks do? Sammy and Jackie and Charles were as much in her now, in a sense, as when she carried them. She would never be free, never be her own person as she was in her youth, before Sam and marriage.

Jackie came to Devon before the sweetbrier bloomed and took Susanna with him to London. "Great things to show you, Mama!"

Great things? "I know this place, yes." She stood studying a ruin on the edge of an abandoned field in by London's Windmill Hill. The foundry. "You know, Jackie, that blew up around the time you left home. There's no roof on it. I certainly hope you got it cheap "

An anthill of workmen ambled about. Stacks of lumber and piles of undressed stone lay haphazardly around the foundry ruin.

The Great London Fire had leveled this particular area, and it had not been rebuilt—yet. True, it was a lovely sort of park, this open hillside on the edge of Moorfields, complete with robust elms. But theaters and bawdyhouses and their attendant base elements were encroaching rapidly on three sides. Open space in this teeming city was becoming a premium. The loveliness was doomed.

"Cheap?" Jackie nodded as he watched the proceedings with a happy satisfaction. "Yes, I got it cheap. Perfect for us; perfect location."

"And how much is the renovation? I think perhaps you were penny wise and pound foolish."

"My estimate says six hundred pounds will build what we want from the ruin. Maybe six fifty. Not a bad price."

"Oh? And what do we want exactly?"

"Charles and I need a headquarters, a base of operations, and the closer the center of town the better. We're fixing an apartment for you upstairs, a place of your own. You can study, write letters, sleep, stare out the window at the elms—whatever your heart desires."

Susanna mulled over the notion. She hadn't really planned beyond living with one daughter or another, perhaps helping out a little with the children. To have rooms just her own sounded appealing. To have them in London more appealing. She ciphered mentally. "Forty-two years."

"What?" Jackie looked at her.

"Forty-two years since I lived in London, and only that one visit back in 'twenty-four. It would be so nice to come back."

She doubted Sammy would approve her living in Charles's and Jackie's headquarters, and she was right. Sammy fussed and fumed and in his pedantic letters called Moorfields a nest of schismatics. Susanna watched her sons at work and kept finding herself with eyebrows raised, secretly wondering if Sammy wasn't right. Jackie and Charles might be ministers in the Church of England, but they certainly weren't conducting either themselves or their services like the average ordained man.

And then in August her life turned around. Perhaps, as she looked back to that moment, it was not her life that turned around, for outwardly she had served God every day she lived. It was the inside of her life.

Her body and thoughts had long put Christ at the beginning and end of each day. Her behavior had paid homage to the God of the universe. But all that—even the thoughts—were in a way simply the outside of her.

She was accepting Communion on a pleasant August afternoon, as she had at least weekly ever since her childhood when she left behind her father's dissenting beliefs and joined the Anglican Church. She knelt as usual, accepted the host as usual, awaited the cup. The familiar priestly intonement came droning along the rail: "The blood of our Lord Jesus Christ, which was shed for thee, preserve thy body and soul unto everlasting life. Drink this in remembrance that Christ's blood was shed for thee, and be thankful."

The cup reached her, she sipped, the cup passed on. *Christ, Christ alone, died for ME.* The familiar words she had heard for fifty-seven years, the liturgy she had memorized, leaped afire and warmed her heart.

Jackie's experience and Charles's flooded her. Her thoughts and actions had always belonged to God. Now for this first time her heart did also. Her warmed heart sang, in this season of the sweetbrier's richest glory, a song to last through the depths of winter.

Suddenly she wanted Sammy to have this wonderful enrichment, this spiritual fulfillment, this inner witness. But he resisted anything not based on rational Scripture study, and, as Sam had always done, when he was certain his position was the right one he would countenance no others. She must phrase her letters carefully, perhaps call in person.

No, letters were the way. Ever since Sammy had left home she had been writing letters to him. Pages and pages. She and Sammy thought alike in many ways. She had never trusted her feelings, not ever; Sam, also. Still, she would try to convey the glory of this experience by letter, although, as Jackie had said, words were inadequate.

But she didn't really have the chance. The son she loved too well died unexpectedly in November at the age of forty-nine.

Jackie's notions were unpopular with a lot of clergy, not just Sammy. The preacher who had adopted itinerant ways found himself preaching to thousands in the open fields, with his mother at his side—and Susanna was proud of it!

She still had to fight those searing bouts with melancholia that weighed her down frequently, but her days saw a constant and satisfying cycle of reading, writing, and listening. She loved the routine, the order, and perhaps most of all the lack of want. No more debt, no more haggling, no more privation.

In March of 1741 Kezzy died in the clergy home Jackie had provided for her. Later Emilia's wandering husband Bob Harper died, making her a widow in fact as well as function.

The spring of 1742 came late, giving a late start to all the blooming and leafing out that makes spring the season of hope. Susanna was seventy-three now. She could feel herself wane, become more frail with each season.

She rarely left her apartment now, but she didn't really have to. Some of the sharpest wits and minds in England came knocking at her door. She enjoyed the company immensely, and she listened with pride to tales of Charles's and Jackie's itinerant preaching.

Sam had dreamed for years of a spiritual revival to come out of Epworth. It was coming—but by the roundabout way of his sons via Oxford and London. They were turning England upside down to the glory of Christ, and Susanna sat happily in the very eye of the storm.

By July, the season of the sweetbrier's full bloom, she was again bedridden, a condition familiar to her. She knew what it was this time, and she asked Nancy to come, and Patty, and Emilia. Charles was here now.

She knew Jackie was in Bristol preaching. Susanna resigned herself to die without his hand in hers. That was all right; his work was important, more important than the passing of an old lady from glory to glory.

Her powers of speech were failing. This servant who always had a word, sharp or soft, would soon be bereft of them. While she could still get words out she asked, "Please, my children, as soon as I'm released, sing a psalm of praise to God."

Strange, this. She could feel life dribbling away, unit by unit—whatever the units of life might be. She had had such difficulty accepting Sam's death, and here she was accepting her own so comfortably. And why not? Her beloved Jesus was taking care of everything.

She recognized the faces keeping watch beside her bed, and her heart sang when she saw Jackie's among them. But her voice and mouth sang no more. She could no longer move at all, but then she felt no need to. Her body was relaxed, her mind serene. Christ could come now anytime. She was ready.

The room opened wide. Wider. The soft light brightened and spread to brilliance. It filled her vision and her soul.

She was home.

Chronology

(Some dates vary slightly according to the source.)

1669—In January, Susanna "Sukey" Annesley is born, last of twenty-five children of leading British dissenter Samuel Annesley.

1682—In August, Susanna at thirteen meets Sam Westley, a student preparing for the dissenting clergy. Susanna changes her religious affiliation from dissenting to Church of England.

1689—Susanna and Sam marry. Sam, too, has espoused the Church of England and has changed his name to Wesley. They set up housekeeping in a small apartment on the Thames. William Prince of Orange and Mary take the throne of England.

1690—In February, Sammy, Jr., is born. At the Battle of the Boyne, William cements his claim to the throne. Sam accepts a position at South Ormsby, a village deep in the wilds of Lincolnshire Wolds.

1691—Their second child, daughter Susanna, comes. The sickly baby dies.

1692—Emilia, their third baby, is born.

1694—Twins, Annesley and Jedediah, die. In December Queen Mary dies of smallpox at thirty-three. The Prince of Orange rules alone.

1695—Their sixth baby, Susanna, nicknamed Sukey, is born. Sammy speaks his first words at age five.

1696—Mary is born. Dubbed Molly, she is permanently maimed by a maid's carelessness.

1697—Sam accepts a larger parish at Epworth, not far from South Ormbsy. There their eighth, Mehetabel, or Hetty, arrives. Over the next five years, five babies, including one set of twins, are born to die.

1701—Sam and Susanna's political convictions regarding the legitimacy of the Prince of Orange come to loggerheads. Sam moves out.

1702—William dies, and Queen Anne accedes to the throne. This fails to end the stubborn political argument that nearly destroys Susanna's marriage. Anne, their fourteenth child, is born and nicknamed Nancy. Susanna and Sam manage to patch their differences and come back together.

1703—John Benjamin Wesley, the fruit of the renewed union, is born and nicknamed Jackie, their fifteenth child.

1704—Sammy, Jr., goes off to school. Political opposition against the Tory Wesleys mounts in this Whig region.

1705—During a raucous political protest outside their house, a nurse accidentally smothers their sixteenth child. Sam is thrown into debtors' prison in Lincoln. John Sharpe, Archbishop of York, comes to his aid at Susanna's behest. Sam will travel to convocations in London for the next seven winters.

1707—Number seventeen, Martha nicknamed Patty, arrives in December. Charles, the eighteenth, is born prematurely and survives.

1709—In February, fire destroys the rectory; Jackie is plucked from a second-story window in a dramatic escape. Kezia (Kezzy), Susanna's nineteenth and last, is born. The children are farmed out until the new brick rectory can be completed.

1711—Susanna begins a winter Sunday evening service in her home, and she must defend it before Sam in the face of complaints by the frightened and jealous curate. The service does much both to promote the gospel and to heal rifts between the locals and their rector. Sam returns to amity.

1714—Jackie goes off to prep school at age eleven. Emilia, twenty-three, goes to Gainsborough to teach.

1715—Sammy, Jr., marries well.

1716—Charles, less than eight, joins his brothers for school in London. Susanna at age forty-seven begins to suffer depressions.

1721—Sukey marries poorly to escape poverty.

1724—For the first time in thirty-five years Susanna returns to London to greet her returning brother. He never arrives, the victim of suspicious circumstance.

1726—Jackie becomes a fellow in Lincoln. During this general period, Hetty runs off with a smooth-talking lawyer who abandons her. She marries William Wright—a most sorry union. Patty goes to London and meets Westley Hall. Sam takes the responsibility for Wroote parish. The arrangement is unsatisfactory and unsuccessful, and Sam eventually moves the family back to Epworth.

1731—Sukey takes ill in November, probably of puerperal fever. Susanna goes to her and herself becomes ill with pleurisy. She begins to suffer overwhelming depression.

1732—An accident leaves Sam slightly disabled. He begins to fade. Westley Hall leaves Patty for Kezzy, returns to Patty and marries her, takes both her and Kezzy back to London.

1735—Sam Wesley dies at age seventy-two. John and Charles go to Georgia to serve as missionaries to the Indians. Susanna lives with Emilia at Gainsborough.

1736—Charles returns from Georgia disillusioned.

1737—John returns a fugitive. The brothers turn their efforts to evangelizing not the Indians but Mother England.

1738—John's Aldersgate conversion shows him an inner witness to salvation, which his father had preached about for years. Charles had received the same several days earlier. Through his sons, the revival Sam, Sr., so long dreamed of finally floods England and the world.

1739—In August, at age seventy, Susanna experiences the same inner witness her husband had described and her sons had found. In November, Sammy, Jr., dies at age forty-nine.

1741—Kezia dies at thirty-two. Emilia's absentee husband, Robert Harper, dies.

1742—At great peace with herself, Susanna goes to meet the Lord she served so faithfully.

Moody Press, a ministry of the Moody Bible Institute, is designed for education, evangelization, and edification. If we may assist you in knowing more about Christ and the Christian life, please write us without obligation: Moody Press, c/o MLM, Chicago, Illinois 60610.